TRAINING DESIGN, DELIVERY, AND DIPLOMACY

Also by A. Keith Young and Tamarra Osborne

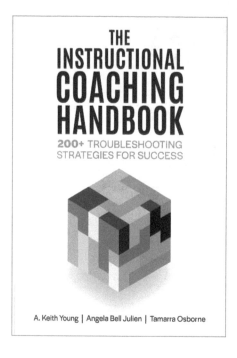

*The Instructional
Coaching Handbook:
200+ Troubleshooting
Strategies for Success*

by A. Keith Young,
Angela Bell Julien,
and Tamarra Osborne

TRAINING DESIGN, DELIVERY, AND DIPLOMACY

An Educator's Guide

A. KEITH YOUNG ■ **TAMARRA OSBORNE**

ascd

Arlington, Virginia USA

2800 Shirlington Rd., Suite 1001 • Arlington, VA 22206 USA
Phone: 800-933-2723 or 703-578-9600 • Fax: 703-575-5400
Website: www.ascd.org • Email: member@ascd.org
Author guidelines: www.ascd.org/write

Richard Culatta, *Chief Executive Officer;* Anthony Rebora, *Chief Content Officer;* Genny Ostertag, *Managing Director, Book Acquisitions and Editing;* Susan Hills, *Senior Acquisitions Editor;* Mary Beth Nielsen, *Director, Book Editing;* Jamie Greene, *Senior Editor;* Thomas Lytle, *Creative Director;* Donald Ely, *Art Director;* Melissa Johnston/The Hatcher Group, *Graphic Designer;* Kelly Marshall, *Production Manager;* Christopher Logan, *Senior Production Specialist;* Cynthia Stock, *Typesetter;* Shajuan Martin, *E-Publishing Specialist*

All web links in this book are correct as of the publication date below but may have become inactive or otherwise modified since that time. If you notice a deactivated or changed link, please email books@ascd.org with the words "Link Update" in the subject line. In your message, please specify the web link, the book title, and the page number on which the link appears.

PAPERBACK ISBN: 978-1-4166-3233-7   ASCD product #124006   n08/23
PDF EBOOK ISBN: 978-1-4166-3234-4; see Books in Print for other formats.
Quantity discounts are available: email programteam@ascd.org or call 800-933-2723, ext. 5773, or 703-575-5773. For desk copies, go to www.ascd.org/deskcopy.

Library of Congress Cataloging-in-Publication Data

Names: Young, A. Keith, author. | Osborne, Tamarra, author.
Title: Training design, delivery, and diplomacy : an educator's guide / A. Keith Young & Tamarra Osborne.
Description: Arlington, VA : ASCD, [2023] | Includes bibliographical references and index.
Identifiers: LCCN 2023018321 (print) | LCCN 2023018322 (ebook) | ISBN 9781416632337 (paperback) | ISBN 9781416632344 (pdf)
Subjects: LCSH: Employees—Training of. | Instructional systems—Design. | Adult education.
Classification: LCC HF5549.5.T7 Y69 2023 (print) | LCC HF5549.5.T7 (ebook) | DDC 658.3/124—dc23/eng/20230614
LC record available at https://lccn.loc.gov/2023018321
LC ebook record available at https://lccn.loc.gov/2023018322

30 29 28 27 26 25 24 23   1 2 3 4 5 6 7 8 9 10 11 12

TRAINING DESIGN, DELIVERY, AND DIPLOMACY

An Educator's Guide

Introduction

This book provides direction for trainers seeking high-leverage strategies for training adults. Additionally, it conveys the essential components of a powerful train-the-trainer program. Read the chapters sequentially or jump to a section where you desire help. For example, is workshop feedback telling you that your training is dry or slow-paced? See Chapter 3: Engaging Participants. Do participants struggle to implement training back in their program or site? If so, study Chapter 1: Training Design to ensure you allocate appropriate practice and how-to information into your training plans.

In short, make the book work for you and your unique situation. We offer numerous strategies; some will work for a particular topic or audience, whereas others will not. If something isn't working, there's always another possibility. Don't be timid about experimenting with a technique you find novel or haven't encountered before. Just as a seasoned cook appreciates and experiments with a well-stocked pantry, you just need to dive in and see what happens. Plan for it, try it out, and then reflect on what you learned from using a new tactic—what works and what doesn't with your personality, attendees, or subject? We frequently work with experienced trainers (including us) who make colossal mistakes. Nevertheless, they still maintain regular invitations to train and receive mountains of positive feedback from the training. What differentiates them is that they're unafraid to experiment, study what happened because of their trials, and then use that information to improve their practice in future training.

Through our work, we have interviewed, observed, and presented with stellar trainers in hundreds of agencies in 28 U.S. states and countries. We conduct workshops for other trainers and coaches, and we observe those same training participants as they implement the practices they learned in training. Most groups with which we work are educational organizations, but some are nonprofits, nongovernmental organizations, and small businesses. In each chapter of this book, you'll find jewels of wisdom and nuts and bolts picked up from a distinguished and diverse group of trainers. We also work with both new and experienced trainers. Consequently, this book addresses and provides tips specific to both audiences. At the end of each section, we include virtual tips for conducting training activities in an online setting.

Regarding the research base behind this book, we believe the primary goal of training is to facilitate participant understanding for the adults (Biech, 2017). John Hattie's work similarly advocated a clear focus on learner outcomes in pedagogy, as did John Biggs and colleagues' research for university learners (Biggs et al., 2022; Hattie, 2023; Hattie & Clarke, 2019). Furthermore, we focus on workshop participants, how they change during training, and how they carry new learning back to work with them. Some presenters focus on being skilled entertainers; by contrast, the most impressive trainers we witness shy away from centering training around their personality and charisma and instead focus on the learning demonstrated by the group. Other extensive works decisively influencing this book include research on instruction from Bell (2021), Saphier (Saphier et al., 2018), and Sherrington (2019).

Chapter 1 includes directions on planning essentials for training adults: setting workshop targets (Biech, 2017; Biggs et al., 2022; Bell, 2021;

Saphier et al., 2018; Sherrington, 2019), determining a learning approach (Archer & Hughes, 2011; Bell, 2021; Saphier et al., 2018; Sherrington, 2019), and planning time. To further enhance training, consider the following design principles: thinking skills (Biggs et al., 2022; Webb, 2002, 2012), tactics to improve the clarity of instruction (Saphier et al., 2018), adult learner characteristics (Biech, 2017; Knowles et al., 2020), trauma considerations (ITTIC, 2015), cultural responsiveness (Chhokar et al., 2019), change theory (Hall & Hord, 2019), and differentiation (Hattie, 2023; NASEM, 2018). Virtual training tips related to designing training are included near the end of the chapter.

The heart of **Chapter 2** concerns decisions made in the spur of the moment. This section helps the trainer promote discussions with equity (Lemov, 2021; Silberman et al., 2015), respond to questions (Hattie & Clarke, 2019; Saphier et al., 2018), provide explicit directions (Garmston, 2018; Lemov, 2021; Saphier et al., 2018), build rapport and trust (Aguilar 2013, 2016; Bloom et al., 2005; Noddings, 2013; Saphier et al., 2018), advocate care (Noddings, 2013), display appropriate body language (Hattie, 2023; Van Edward, 2017), and address nervousness (Biech, 2017; Damisch et al., 2010). Strategies for implementing some of these ideas during online training appear at the end of the chapter.

A vast body of research provides the unrelenting need for learners to actively participate in their learning journey; this principle operates for both children and adults (Archer & Hughes, 2011; Biech, 2017; Biggs et al., 2022; Darling-Hammond et al., 2020; Mroz et al., 2018; NASEM, 2018; Saphier et al., 2018; Wammes et al., 2019). **Chapter 3** supplies 50 methods for promoting engagement in training, which demonstrate ways to involve adults through writing, speaking, demonstrating, and active listening. Read what researchers recommend about maintaining engagement throughout workshops and considerations for participants in virtual training.

Chapter 4 addresses many trainers' concerns about working with adults, receiving challenging reactions, and preparing diplomatic responses. The practical application of positive intent receives clear-cut attention (Bailey, 2011, 2015; Costa et al., 2016; Curwin et al., 2018;

Noddings, 2013; Patterson et al., 2021). Tips for listening are offered (Costa et al., 2016; Dumbro et al., 2020; Knowles et al., 2020; Van Edward, 2017), along with more than 35 approaches for managing challenging behaviors (Aguilar, 2016; Gordon & Burch, 2010; Knowles et al., 2020; Mroz et al., 2018; Young et al., 2023). As with the other chapters, virtual considerations for problematic behaviors emerge at the end of the chapter.

Finally, **Chapter 5** answers the question we are frequently asked: How do you structure such successful train-the-trainer programs? We took a few decades of expertise in creating impactful train-the-trainer initiatives and combined it with research on effective instruction (Archer & Hughes, 2011; Bell, 2021; Saphier et al., 2018; Sherrington, 2019) and research reviews on other train-the-trainer programs for classroom management, special education services, school improvement, and health professionals (Jones et al., 1977; LaVigna et al., 2005; Pearce et al., 2012; Pollnow, 2012; Suhrheinrich, 2014). The Young-Osborne Train-the-Trainer Model is provided in this chapter, along with detailed tips for soliciting new trainers' best practices, maintaining the training program's accuracy, and attending to budget and time constraints. Having completed several virtual train-the-trainer programs, we also provide virtual strategies to consider.

1

Training Design

Most often, a room that is pleasing to the eye contains a robust design. Interior designers plan rooms based on established design principles and carefully consider the possibilities of, for example, a colossal textile overwhelming a piece of furniture or juxtaposing colors and proportions to achieve balance or rhythm. Likewise, a high-quality training session must be planned with a thoughtful design and take multiple possible results into consideration.

This chapter includes our best tips and research guidance for the essentials of training adults: setting workshop goals (Biech, 2017; Biggs et al., 2022; Bell, 2021; Saphier et al., 2018; Sherrington, 2019), identifying a learning approach (Archer & Hughes, 2011; Bell, 2021, Saphier et al., 2018; Sherrington, 2019), budgeting time, managing adult learners' needs (Biech, 2017; Knowles et al., 2020), and evaluating results. For experienced trainers looking to elevate their training to the next level, consider the following design components in this chapter: thinking skills (Biggs et al., 2022; Webb, 2002, 2012), clarity devices (Saphier et al., 2018), trauma considerations (ITTIC, 2015), cultural sensitivity (Chhokar et al., 2019), the change process (Hall & Hord, 2019), and differentiation (Hattie, 2023;

NASEM, 2018). For training limitations and techniques for planning virtual training, skip to the end of this chapter. If you're providing predesigned training that you do not need to design, you might want to jump to Chapter 3 for ideas that provide more interaction in traditional workshops or presentations.

Training Basics

Early in his teaching career, a coach chatted with Keith after observing him lead a very engaging middle school lesson. After some discussion about strengths and highlights of the class, the coach asked, "What were students able to do when they walked out the door that they couldn't do when they came in your classroom?"

Keith was stumped. Until then, he had assumed that as students worked their way through a series of appealing activities, they would just pick up the intended learning. Thanks to the observant coach, though, Keith started thinking about lesson outcomes. Emerging from this experience and with decades of practice under their belts, Keith and Tamarra honed their collective skill, focusing on learner outcomes when planning training. Further, they combined this approach with constructed alignment—carefully aligning teaching and assessment to intended learning outcomes—as advocated for university instructors (Biggs et al., 2022) and instructional processes detailed by several others (Biech, 2017; Bell, 2021; Lemov, 2021; Saphier et al., 2018; Sherrington, 2019).

When planning training, it's important to ask yourself, "What will participants walk away from the training able to do that they couldn't do (or couldn't do well) beforehand?" Write down your answer and use it to guide the remainder of Chapter 1 and your training planning.

Once you have the desired outcome in hand, decide if there's enough time for participants to reach the goal during the training you have planned. If not, consider

- Increasing the training time.
- Breaking the training into a series of discrete events.
- Incorporating other forms of learning for adults, such as a book study, action research, team planning, coaching, or a job aide. For other powerful alternatives to training, see Biech (2017), Easton

(2015), Knowles et al. (2020), and NASEM (2018). Remember, training is only one format for educator learning.

Whatever you do, try to avoid cramming multiple days of learning into just a couple hours and then blaming "lack of time" for a lack of comprehension from the participants. You won't know if anyone learned anything just because they sat, stared at you, and applauded afterward. We contend that if you want people to actually learn something—even something complex and conceptual—they need to *show* what they learned. Ideally, they must show that learning before leaving the training room. In Chapter 3, we explore several ways of efficiently achieving this goal of "showing you before they leave the training." For now, let's take a look at setting clear learning outcomes from the get-go.

Set Clear Goals

Once you've written down what participants need to demonstrate before they walk out the door, turn that goal into a statement with an observable, measurable verb. The instructional team at WestEd (2016) recommended a handful of concrete verbs for learner outcomes: *write*, *draw*, *speak*, and *perform*. Almost every learning target imaginable can be phrased as an observable, measurable action. To illustrate, let's say you want to see how well people can drive a car or bake a biscuit—not how well they listen to a lecture about driving or baking. What is a reasonable way for participants to display this new learning? How close can you get to approximating the skill in a training setting?

They might write a plan incorporating a theory, tell someone their understanding of a concept, or apply a rule by writing an evaluation or practicing a conversation. In each of these examples, they need to write, speak, or perform. When you cast your goal as a measurable action, avoid more traditional, illusive actions such as *know*, *identify*, *learn*, and *understand*. These words often lead to vague outcomes that are not actually measured (or truly measurable) in or after training. If you asked 14 trainers for their definition of what it means to *know* something, you're likely to get at least 12 different answers. Does *knowing* something mean you can simply repeat back what was learned in training? Or does it require you to produce the new learning in a work environment?

With your goal clearly in mind, post it at the top of your planning notes or computer screen and edit *every activity* to ensure participants move toward that goal. If you're not confident an activity moves people toward your intended destination, replace it with one that does. Dynamic trainers embody strong instructional *and* editorial skills. It's important to post and communicate the goal during all training sessions; this action adds clarity and intention to all workshop activities, one of the surest ways to positively affect learning attainment (Bell, 2021; Hattie, 2023; Hattie & Clarke, 2019; Saphier et al., 2018; Sherrington, 2019).

Plan for Explicit Instruction or Constructed Knowledge

If you're working with procedural knowledge, routines, or foundational skills people need to learn, then you might want to stick with explicit instruction. Training on implementing a curriculum, conducting an assessment, and following a routine procedure are topics well suited for explicit instruction. More conceptual information—abstractions, schemata, and mental models—is often best transmitted via constructed learning: knowledge that usually occurs via an activity that causes participants to explore a model, problem, or case study for a set of attributes or criteria. With the constructed knowledge approach, the trainer provides guiding questions to move people through a specific discovery. Reaching the intended outcome depends on the participants' prior knowledge or experiences related to the new learning (Bell, 2021; Biggs et al., 2022; Knowles et al., 2020; Saphier, 2017; Sherrington, 2019). Therefore, providing multiple examples and nonexamples of appropriate syllabi, for example, while instructors cull a set of guidelines or a rubric for a well-written course syllabus empowers them to write a precise course outline on their own.

> **Expert**
>
> Remember that not every workshop or skill requires concept development. If there is one way to do something, then explicit instruction is typically the best way to teach it. Vet your instructional approach based on the knowledge or skills your participants need by the end of training.

Explicit instruction and constructed knowledge possess both advantages and disadvantages. Typically, explicit instruction works well in short bursts; it is effective for building foundational knowledge or training on a routine procedure. By contrast, constructed knowledge proves challenging to form without prior knowledge of a topic. You must find a way to develop or access knowledge needed for new learning with constructed knowledge, which takes time. In the previous example about syllabus building, for the constructed knowledge approach to work, the participants would need to review multiple models and nonexamples before extracting a comprehensive set of generalizable guidelines. At the same time, if folks must understand something at the conceptual level or break an ingrained ineffective habit, then constructed knowledge training is often most appropriate. Additionally, it's been shown that constructed knowledge generally lasts longer than knowledge gained through explicit instruction (Social Programs That Work, 2021).

Novice

If you're struggling to develop training based on concept attainment, then target a series of skill-building workshops. Then, as you gain more confidence working with adults, experiment with smaller activities that are focused on building conceptual knowledge.

Map Out Your Training Time

Once you've determined the approach to learning you'll take in the training—constructed or explicit—take a look at one way to design training so it focuses on participants' outcomes. Consider chunking training times and applying the following ideas:

1. Start planning in reverse, and detail the final product, procedure, or skill first.
2. Then do some structural planning for how you and the participants practice the product, process, or skill together.
3. Finally, design a strategy whereby you'll model or explain the final product (or lead a discovery activity in the case of a constructed knowledge workshop).

This backward-planning approach focuses on what attendees walk out the door with that they didn't have before the workshop. As a result, the trainer ends up with the classic "I do, we do, you do" format. For workshops using constructed knowledge, keep the initial goals broader than explicit instruction objectives; folks need time and flexibility to indirectly uncover the new learning. You also need to schedule more time for the actual discovery activity since you may need to build appropriate background knowledge. Figure 1.1 illustrates these two approaches.

As you plan your schedule, there are a few pitfalls expert trainers tend to avoid. First, make the opening brief. Instead of spending a massive amount of time on one lengthy community builder or extensive introductions, plan a brief activity directly connected to the targeted learning. This is also called an activator (Saphier et al., 2018). We observed a chemistry teacher lead a workshop for other science educators who did not know one another. The training topic included an innovative way to learn the periodic table. The trainer opened the workshop by simply asking folks to locate three new people, introduce themselves, and explain how they currently teach the periodic table. As a result, participants formed small personal connections and activated their current knowledge about the day's learning. This is a great example of an activator—a simple community builder that also activates prior knowledge. A tip to consider as you plan training involves sprinkling tiny community builders throughout the workshop as people join new partners or small groups to complete tasks. The start of a workshop is not the only time you can (or should) address relationship building in training.

Novice

Be cautious of spending too much time with team-building activities or overexplaining during the opening of the workshop. You should literally plan your training minute by minute the first few times until you get into the habit of allocating most of the time to the instructional model, concept development, or participant practice.

FIGURE 1.1

Workshop Time Allocations

Explicit Instruction		Constructed Knowledge	
Time Allotted	**Training Section**	**Time Allotted**	**Training Section**
5%	The trainer provides an opening, introductions, a community builder/ activator, and workshop goals.	5%	The trainer provides an opening, introductions, a community builder/activator, and workshop goals.
30%	The trainer explains, represents, or models the final concept, skill, or attitude (i.e., "I do").	60%	• Using guiding questions, the trainer leads a discovery activity that targets the desired concept, skill, or attitude. • Participants connect new information to prior knowledge. Alternatively, pertinent background information is developed as part of the activity. • The trainer shares a model if participants fail to construct the new learning adequately through the discovery activity. ("We do" and "I do" are conducted as needed with the whole group at this point.)
30%	Participants practice a version of the final product *with* the trainer and receive feedback (i.e., "We do").		
30%	• Participants perform, speak, or write the workshop goal independently or in small groups and plan for implementation following training (i.e., "You do"). • The trainer works with a small group that needs more support or enrichment (i.e., "We do").	30%	• Participants perform, speak, or write the workshop goal independently or in small groups and plan for implementation following training (i.e., "You do"). • The trainer works with a small group that needs more support or enrichment (i.e., "We do").
5%	The trainer conducts a summarizing activity and communicates follow-up expectations.	5%	The trainer conducts a summarizing activity and communicates follow-up expectations.

The second potential pitfall regarding time involves practice. Skilled trainers never shortcut participant practice. Practice and action planning in small groups allow the trainer to check and see if the new learning will potentially stick (Lemov et al., 2012). In addition, savvy trainers use this time to correct errors or reinforce concepts as needed. (Find more structures for participant practice in Chapter 3.)

Setting clear goals, planning for constructed knowledge or explicit instruction, and mapping out your training time are workshop essentials; they're the steps that comprise the primary training structure. However, preparation doesn't end there. Just as basic pieces in a wardrobe are enhanced and made more functional with accessories and other complementary additions, your training, participants' thinking, and the learning environment can be enriched with a bit more work, which is detailed in the following sections.

Training Premiums

Even though adults learn much like any other age group, they possess unique characteristics that differ slightly from other learners, such as adolescents or toddlers (Biech, 2017; Knowles et al., 2020; NASEM, 2018). Based on our experience and observations of several champion trainers, three adult learning needs continually stand out as crucial to the successful training of adult learners: providing practical knowledge, connecting training to prior experience, and providing alternatives. In the following sections, we discuss the factors that influence adult learners and provide practical ways to address those needs in training.

Provide How-To Information

Adults tend to be driven to learn information intended to solve work or life problems (Biech, 2017; Knowles et al., 2020; NASEM, 2018). To address this need, consider how-to information when planning your training. For example, in a workshop goal, you might write, "Today, you'll demonstrate five steps for ____" or "In the next hour, you'll write a plan for solving ____."

Most adults crave this kind of practical implementation information. However, some attendees may seek out the pertinent theories or research, so know the research behind your training subject matter and be prepared to share it as needed (while keeping the training focused on practical information). Even if the training is about philosophy or theory, dig deep in planning and find a way to ensure participants know how to apply the theoretical ideas in a meaningful manner. For example, a goal involving theoretical information could be "You'll demonstrate understanding of sociobiology by writing a plan to use the theory in a lab setting."

Expert

Be careful not to carry on for too long about the research base behind your training. Know the research, reference it, and build your workshop around it, but ensure a majority of participants and a major portion of the training time focus on how to implement what you're talking about in a practical way. One way to do this is to consider every possible issue that might go wrong with the implementation of a theory or concept your training is about. Then find a way to address those concerns during training so the theoretical becomes practical.

Occasionally, people ask us to review their training because they received negative feedback from participants. Most of the time, we find one of two components missing. Either (1) there were not enough practical, implementable ideas, or (2) there was not enough adult engagement, and the training primarily provided a series of slides that were read to the crowd. We address the issue of low participant engagement in Chapter 3, but the former error suggests that the trainer needs to seriously think about how the training topic translates to the work environment. For example, it is often insufficient to tell teachers to maintain positive relationships with students to improve classroom management—without providing realistic approaches to accomplishing this. Training in this case must address what to do with unresponsive students. What do you do when students' values conflict with yours? Among 120 students, whom do you target first for relationship building?

Multiple considerations about implementation inevitably arise in most training topics, so focus on the most common ones. Adults need helpful information for common implementation issues or, at the very least, further resources to consult. Training that is focused on real-life, practical information helps preclude challenging behaviors from adult participants and increases the likelihood that participants carry the workshop learning back to their jobs.

Appreciate Adults' Experiences

Adults bring a great deal of experience with them. It is imperative to respect and draw on their backgrounds when their experiences relate to the workshop goals. Even when a participant's past practice doesn't align with new learning, appreciate it nonetheless since adults integrate new information by comparing it with their own experiences (Knowles et al., 2020; NASEM, 2018). In many respects, adults consider their own experiences to be as valuable as the trainer's background (or any body of research). This belief can be helpful in training if the learner is reflective and their experiences inform the new learning in a supportive way. On the other hand, training may be more challenging if the new knowledge directly opposes their experience. Chapter 4 offers ideas to help integrate and respect participants' experiences, which may collide with workshop goals.

Provide Choices

Adults like control, which is why self-directed learning remains a hallmark of adult education (Biech, 2017; Knowles et al., 2020; NASEM, 2018). Primarily, most adults are internally motivated and see themselves as equal to their instructors in terms of authority. Help them control their learning during training by having them set personal goals or create specific action plans for implementation following the training. If possible, solicit participants' input before training to help in the initial design. Ask them what they know and need to know about the upcoming topic. Then reference the collected data throughout the training and provide options during training. For example, "Do you want to conduct this activity individually or with a partner? You decide." Continue to solicit input during and after workshops. Check in with participants during breaks for reactions to activities, workshop pacing, or time for activities. When possible, allow participants to make these simple choices: select your seat, pick your partner, vote on the group's lunchtime, choose what part of a plan to work on first. Simple tactics such as these help provide attendees with choices, control, and power that are applicable in the workshop environment.

Expert

Providing stations or more than one activity for each learning objective offers effective choices for adults in the workshop setting. Do you have two activities for reaching a learning goal but can't decide which to use? In this case, consider explaining both in training and letting the adults select which one they want to complete. Maybe some folks want to read about how another teacher implemented a strategy while a small group wants to complete the simulation or role-play that same strategy. Both ideas can be options in the training.

Evaluate the Training

Include an evaluation of the training in your design (Biech, 2017). Try to avoid focusing the evaluation too much on surface-level training conditions (e.g., How was the room temperature? How did you feel about the day? Did the trainer address your needs?). Although some of this information can be valuable, it's more important to focus on what participants learned and how they plan to implement what they learned. Be clear about what you are assessing; you'll likely gain critical but imprecise feedback if your evaluation questions are too open-ended. Are you looking for organizational change? Do you need an assessment of individual skills or concept attainment? Your assessment should be consistent with your workshop goals, so make sure you're assessing the change you want to see.

We like to keep our feedback form short and allow time during the training to complete it so more folks actually provide data. Typically, we ask what the most valuable part of the training was, what workshop goals or skills folks plan to implement from the training, and what people would change about the workshop. Surface-level feedback (e.g., if the sound in the room was awful or if the trainer was rude) is typically shared with the last question. Many seasoned trainers ask for questions left unanswered at the end of training. Analyzing trend data from the surveys and reviewing action plans people intend to implement after training are two ways to infer what is most likely to be transferred back to the worksite.

> **Expert**
>
> Kick your evaluation up a notch by planning to see implementation. Participants may lose a great deal of detail between training and application back at the work site. When possible, use your influence to build some type of observation follow-up into the initial training design.

Don't forget to collect formative data as you move throughout the workshop. Ask for brief written feedback after a significant activity. Conduct a short quiz after you present a model and before practice to determine who gained the concept and who didn't. Collect anecdotal notes as you move among small teams. Take photographs of work products or action plans drafted in the workshop. The final evaluation should not provide too many surprises if you collect tiny data samples throughout the training. Combine this formative data with your final evaluation to inform what strategies you might use as you move forward.

Move Training to the Next Level

Webb's Depth of Knowledge (DoK) (Webb, 2002, 2012) provides a framework—similar to Bloom's taxonomy (Anderson & Krathwohl, 2001)—to check the workshop objective or goal against the type of thinking sought from participants. If you want folks to demonstrate comprehension or hope to increase the likelihood that they'll apply what they learned, you need to plan activities that solicit thinking at a more complex level than simply repeating back what they learned. Use the guide in Figure 1.2 to help craft a training plan and activities.

There is a fourth level to Webb's framework; it is like DoK 3 but involves more lengthy work and, potentially, multiple resources (Webb,

FIGURE 1.2

Depth of Knowledge (DoK) Levels of Thinking for Workshops

Type of Thinking	Workshop Outcome Examples	
DoK Level 1		
Participants simply recall facts, terms, steps, simple procedures, or concept definitions. In the end, participants give the information back in a format similar to how it was presented during the workshop.	• Participants write the methods for applying _____ theory. • Today, you'll demonstrate the three steps in dealing with challenging situations. • Today, you'll write three things you learned about teamwork.	Typically, participants provide only one correct response or example to show their understanding at DoK Levels 1 and 2. There is one right way to show the workshop outcome.
DoK Level 2		
Participants apply DoK 1 types of information. Alternatively, participants complete procedures more complex than DoK 1 information that requires a degree of decision making. Participants reproduce the information in their own words through simple role plays, quizzes, writing, etc., by the end of training.	• Today, your job is to write a comparison between the old policy and the new policy. • People perform a role play using the five principles of listening covered today. • Participants will sort relevant and nonrelevant data according to the criteria provided.	
DoK Level 3		
• Originate a plan to approach a problem. • Employ decision making and justification. • Solve abstract, complex, or nonroutine issues. Participants add some of their ideas connected to the workshop information and produce a unique outcome using the attributes above. Some type of careful analysis occurs at this level.	• Participants conduct a role play _deciding between and justifying_ the best approaches learned today. • Each person writes an action plan specific to their work context, using the guidelines provided in training. • Participants write an analysis of three research articles and select findings to include in their work plans.	At DoK Level 3, there is more than one way for participants to complete the training outcome correctly. Multiple unique responses may be correct.

Note: These three levels are adapted from the four levels of Webb's Depth of Knowledge (Webb, 2002, 2012).

2002, 2012). Think of completing an extensive research project, conducting a complex science lab, or forming and constructing a set design for a play, and you'll have an idea of what DoK 4 looks like. For most workshop timeframes, DoK 3 is the most complex thinking necessary—or practical.

Training for thinking at DoK 4 requires multiple sessions completed over time and all the components involved for thinking at DoK 3. At a minimum, you want to obtain DoK 2 in terms of results; at this level, participants show they maintain a comprehensive, if not unique, understanding of the workshop content.

Novice

Start your training design with the intention for participants to produce work at DoK 2. With more training experience, begin to target goals at DoK 3.

Plan for Clarity Edits

Clarity in training pertains to the trainer's ability to get into participants' heads in a way that provides learning comprehension. The following are various tools to consider when planning training, which we call clarity edits. Pick and choose to best match your situation, content, or goal. The concept of clarity is couched in terms of edits because most of us need to revise our workshop activities out of necessity and with an eye for precision; we often underexplain or overgild workshop activities. Highly experienced trainers tell us their most significant training improvements arrived when they started removing unnecessary workshop activities, graphics, or decorations with an eye for which components were most crucial to move the learners toward the learning goals. In other words, they stopped "gilding the lily" of their workshops. Similarly, paying more careful attention to explaining key concepts with thoughtful illustrations, anecdotes, or tasks led to equally valuable edits to training.

Novice

Write in your presenter notes why you're doing the activity. Use your notes to communicate activity rationales throughout training. This action helps the adults comprehend the learning more thoroughly, and it may help you in the design phase to determine if activities need to be removed from the workshop.

Edit activities for clarity. It bears mentioning again that training tasks must move participants efficiently toward the final product or thinking they're expected to show. Some concepts need a presenter model, others call for a video sample, and still others might merit group discussion. However, simply injecting superfluous videos, games, simulations, or other content into a workshop increases the likelihood of learner confusion. Both Hattie (2023) and Saphier and colleagues (2018) vigorously advocate for alignment and communication of learning targets with learning activities to provide clarity of instruction. Throughout training, explain how each activity is designed to move people closer to the final goal; even something as simple as a whole-group chat needs a clear goal or rationale (Watson & Busch, 2021).

Expert

Edit, edit, edit. One of the biggest issues we note with highly experienced trainers involves their propensity to include too many activities in their workshops. Just because you love an activity, have used it successfully for many years, and participants respond well to it does not mean it is *necessary* in order for folks to learn in every workshop.

Edit visuals for clarity. Which handouts, slides, and technologies communicate the learning essentials? Do you include a slide show just because everyone else does? Don't be tempted to cram a great deal of text into one or two presentation slides; the struggle to track and comprehend spoken words with heavy text is why many folks find slideshow presentations boring (Koch et al., 2020). If you're going to provide dense reading material, it's a good idea to print it out in a readable font or offer it electronically, along with room on the page for folks to take notes. Match the materials you use to the goal of the activity. Not every workshop needs a slide deck, poster chart activity, or handout in order for learning to occur.

In order to use visuals intentionally, you'll want to spend some time studying design principles in visual arts (Malamed, 2015) and the power of visuals and graphics that are congruent to and help explain text (Schmeck

Novice

Study the essentials of visual design. Just because you've viewed slide show presentations for years as a student and teacher doesn't mean those slide decks adhered to our current understanding of effective design.

et al., 2014; Watson & Busch, 2021). Once you have a grasp of effective design principles, you can couple visuals with the most appropriate teaching tools, whether it's a slide deck, physical model, chart, bookmark, job aide, booklet, or another format. Consider how you can provide the least amount of information necessary for participants to understand—and resist the urge to add more (Hale & Grenny, 2020). Experiment with drawing visuals live during training (in lieu of preproducing graphics for handouts and slides). Researchers revealed that learners retain more information when they observe their instructors draw and create in front of them (Fiorella & Mayer, 2016).

Expert

Try conducting a full training without a slide presentation. You may need to find a way to include complex directions in your handout packet or on a projected document, but see if you can do that without a full presentation deck. This slide-free trial may force you to view your presentation skills from a new and more interactive angle. At the same time, consider how this tactic might adversely affect your participants if they are English language learners.

Edit stories for clarity. Just because you find it funny or moving doesn't mean a story is a great match for training. Think of anecdotes and analogies like spices; you need to use them judiciously to stimulate and enhance the learning experience—to add clarity (Saphier et al., 2018). In his trainings, Keith often included a personal story about toe surgery, which seemed appropriately graphic and humorous to illustrate a point about learning. Long after one workshop, he encountered a former participant who went on and on about how engaging Keith's training was and how delightfully they recalled the toe surgery story. Keith casually asked *why* the story was included in the training. The enthusiast replied, "Oh, I have no idea, but it was the best story!" Flummoxed, Keith learned a lesson about editing stories and analogies. Some might argue this story still served a purpose since it was so memorable—the participant remembered the training. That said, being memorable isn't enough for high-quality learning; people need to retain the content, skill, or rationale behind the story for the primary learning to be of lasting value.

Nowadays, we consider two issues with storytelling. First, does the parable efficiently move participants toward the learning goal? Is it indispensable? Second, sandwich the story within three steps:

1. Tell people why you are telling the story.
2. Tell the story.
3. Tell people why you told the story.

In an effort to make the story stick, we often make participants repeat the rationale for the story aloud. A tale wrapped in an explanatory bun helps convey the story's point.

Expert

> Edit your stories. A concern for highly experienced trainers involves the sheer number of stories you have. Make sure you're not too focused on the number of stories you provide. Select stories judiciously to make your points.

Edit the environment for clarity. Match the room arrangement to your workshop goals (Saphier et al., 2018). Is one of your subgoals group cohesiveness and cooperative learning? Then construct small groups and provide materials that require sharing. Do you need to check individual progress during training? Then make sure you have the space to circulate and check participants' work. Are you incorporating small groups or station work? Then plan for the furniture to support that goal. Will a tabletop piled high with children's toys propel the learning forward? If yes, then by all means, include the playthings. If not, remove them from the space. Is music necessary to help participants achieve the goal? If not, drop it; the impact of general background music on learning revealed an unfavorable effect. In fact, most researchers recommend leaving music out of training entirely (Biech, 2017; Moreno & Mayer, 2000; Watson & Busch, 2021).

Edit your speech for clarity. In general, you need to speak in a strong voice and use a microphone even when you think you don't need to. Avoid the use of undefined acronyms and jargon (e.g., PLC, SIP, FOMO). If using a specific term proves central to the workshop, then provide a precise and clearly cited definition. Even among educators, we continue to find tremendous variances in how people define everyday concepts such as *mastery, analysis,* and *formative assessment.* The savvy trainer includes cited definitions for key terms at every available opportunity. See Chapter 4 for why this idea might preclude some challenging behaviors from adults in training.

Manage the Change Process

Although multiple theories about the change process exist, we prefer the Concerns-Based Adoption Model of Change (CBAM) offered by Hall and Hord (2019), which communicates the need to consider individuals' apprehensions as they move through change. Generally speaking, people's first concerns about change revolve around basic details: *What is the new change?* The second set of worries involves how the change affects the individual and their work. The final concerns involve the outcomes of the change and how the process might be modified or improved. See Figure 1.3 for a visual representation of how we adapted the seven stages of CBAM into a straightforward approach to training planning.

How does knowing CBAM (or any other change model) affect training? Understanding that people move through discrete stages of change and that some people can get stuck in one stage proves imperative to training design. In addition, understanding the change process allows you to anticipate problems as you plan training and manage expectations. Typically, collaboration about a change occurs after individuals receive all the essential information and their initial concerns are fully addressed. One quick way that experienced trainers determine where people are

FIGURE 1.3

Stages of Change: CBAM Adapted for Training

General Stages of Concern	Typical Participant Questions
With the onset of a new change, people are concerned about basic terminology and facts regarding the issue or idea.	• What is this called? • When does it start? • Is there funding for this? • Aren't we already doing this? • Why are we doing this?
As folks move through the process of a change, they start to be interested in how the change affects them directly: their responsibilities, time required, deadlines, and so on.	• How do I match this to my required schedule? • Will I be paid more for this expectation? • Is it going to affect my current line of courses?
Finally, as people become comfortable with the change, they become more curious about outcomes that result from the change, interested in collaboration with others experiencing the same issue, and thoughtful about how the entire process might be improved.	• How does this affect student outcomes? • Is there a social network site for this initiative? • Can we tweak the implementation of this initiative now? • Is this more efficient than our current program?

Note: These stages are adapted from Hall and Hord's (2019) seven levels of concern people have as they progress through change.

(regarding the stages of concern) involves conducting a brief survey in which they ask, "What are your questions regarding _____ [the new initiative or learning]?" With the data in hand, they match the responses to one of the three stages in Figure 1.3. That data reveal where the trainer focuses most of the training structure—basic information, personal impact issues, collaboration, or refinement.

Novice

When introducing a new concept to educators, don't expect participants to produce in-depth group work on the topic from the get-go. If you want synergistic teamwork, ensure beforehand that most folks know the essential components of a new idea and that their personal concerns are (at least minimally) addressed.

Be Trauma-Informed

Many adults have experienced trauma, and there are ways to structure training to be sensitive to that. Consider the five principles of trauma-informed care (ITTIC, 2015) and find ways to build them into your training design. Keep in mind that many aspects of trauma-informed presentations overlap with the essential characteristics of adult learners (Biech, 2017; Knowles et al., 2020; NASEM, 2018) and how adults experience the change process (Hall & Hord, 2019).

Safety. Safety includes physical and emotional security. If you expect participants to model something live for the whole group, for example, make sure you ask permission and gauge comfort levels before the training begins. If activities involve role play and practice in front of others, clearly communicate this expectation as a requirement before training. Ensure people know with whom you might share information regarding comments and behavior in training. Let people know they can take breaks as needed to address personal issues.

Choice. When reasonable, provide options. Consider allowing people to decide where to sit or which group to join. Especially if the training wasn't optional for someone, it's important to include as many choices as possible during training. Having options is a primary characteristic of adult learning *and* trauma-informed practice. Think about letting people complete tasks individually or with a small group or partner. Consider practical alternatives to achieving the same workshop outcomes, and offer those options throughout training. If someone doesn't want to engage in a simulation, think of another way they might demonstrate the new learning.

Novice

After completing your training plan, review it. Look for opportunities to build in choice throughout the training. Ask yourself, "Can folks do something besides write at this point? What is another way participants might show me their learning? Can I provide two or three different activities for the same training outcome?"

Collaboration. Include and utilize collaborative strategies. Solicit feedback as you move through the workshop. Ask participants to let you know how the workshop pacing feels to them. Check in with individuals and small groups, and ask how they're receiving the day's information. Ask what might be improved. Make any sensible adjustments on the spot; don't wait for the end-of-workshop evaluations to make easy changes. Remember to collaborate with participants before the training through surveys and during the training with formal and informal feedback.

Trustworthiness. Dependability and credibility are crucial to trauma-informed training. Be clear about norms and expectations, don't violate them, and intervene if participants break the agreements. Set clear boundaries for discussion topics, and communicate why you are asking the questions you are asking (Watson & Busch, 2021), along with your intention behind each workshop activity, video, and set of questions.

Empowerment. Help people feel self-determined. Focus on strategies that empower participants while they learn new information. For example, let folks know how the content is practical and will make their work more efficient. As participants practice (and during other pertinent times of feedback), praise their efforts at improvement and self-examination.

Be Culturally Sensitive

Check your training design in terms of cultural sensitivity. The Global Leadership and Organizational Behavior Effectiveness project (GLOBE) provided the most comprehensive study of societal differences in leadership, trust, and culture from more than 500 researchers in over 160 countries (Chhokar et al., 2019; House et al., 2014). See Figure 1.4 for a summary of GLOBE's culture dimensions.

This study revealed values that crossed several cultures. For example, almost all groups showed a preference for participative leadership and employee involvement in decision making. Additionally, multiple cultures value excellence, high standards, innovation, and equitable power. Unequal distribution of power proved less desirable among most societies. For trainers, it is essential to know your values and how they influence

FIGURE 1.4

Summary of GLOBE's Culture Dimensions

Future orientation is the value of gratification delay and future planning.	**Performance orientation** is the degree to which innovation, standards, and exceptional performance are valued.	**Uncertainty avoidance** is about how comfortable people are with risk, change, and ambiguity.
Human orientation is the degree to which fairness, altruism, and kindness are valued.	**Assertiveness** is the degree to which individuals use force and confrontation.	**Power distance** is the extent to which people accept an unequal distribution of power.
Institutional collectivism is the degree to which individuals distribute resources and take collective action.	**In-group collectivism** is the degree to which individuals value loyalty and cohesion to groups and families.	**Gender equality** is the degree to which female and male equality is valued.

the learning goals of the workshop. We highly recommend these additional resources for trainers working on culturally sensitive training: Hammond's *Culturally Responsive Teaching and the Brain* (2015), Ladson-Billings's *Culturally Relevant Pedagogy* (2021), and the NASEM's *How People Learn II* (2018).

Experienced trainers let people know when their values may directly contrast with their own. For example, Tamarra conducted early childhood training in a region where it was culturally acceptable for toddlers and preschoolers to receive spankings as a form of discipline in childcare programs. Likewise, the behaviors Tamarra understood as representative of typical childhood development—expressing anger or disagreement—were perceived by several attendees as evidence of immorality or conscience defiance. In an attempt to find common ground and understanding, Tamarra explained her personal beliefs about assertiveness and the extent to which physical force should not be used against children by care providers. Her ideas conflicted with some participants' values, but despite this ideological conflict, Tamarra's calm clarification helped the group attend to the remaining training content and remain open to her philosophy of early care.

Differentiate

Whenever possible, tailor your training to accommodate various individual preferences. One of the most common complaints we hear from training participants concerns the lack of differentiated training for those who are already familiar with the content and those who are still novices. Address this issue as you design and develop your workshops. If you know the group, conduct a brief assessment to determine their experience levels and expertise with the content, and then plan accordingly. If you can't determine the group's experience in advance, try to plan a few options that are built in to the training. For example, if you're reviewing research with teachers from several different levels, provide a range of studies on the same topic that are appropriate for the different ages or content areas.

Remember to distinguish your training approach for both novice and experienced adults. Frequently, highly skilled participants may be more concerned with the conceptual framework or rationale behind an idea. With this in mind, be prepared to present these professionals with thorough research and ample justification. The need for thorough justification is often why experts benefit from an overexplanation of concepts (Hattie, 2018). Additionally, with their more extensive background, veterans often need help focusing on *when* and *with whom* they should apply a new technique (Knowles et al., 2020; NASEM, 2018). With their more extensive experience, typically, the pros get the "what and why" of new ideas fairly quickly. Then, they often move to implementation without carefully thinking through when and where the new idea might work best. It may seem counterintuitive to get the expert to slow down and contemplate implementation, but that is precisely what they need; work with them more carefully on how they plan to apply new skills and ideas.

On the other hand, novice professionals may be distracted by too much information and benefit from descriptions with minimal elaboration (Hattie, 2023; NASEM, 2018). They often need procedural matters addressed thoroughly because they frequently struggle to retrieve the massive amounts of information required in new work. They also usually take more time to think through issues and put actions into place (NASEM, 2018). Novice educators often need more practice rounds to pick up new techniques. Therefore, it's a good idea to consider breaking people into affinity groups of novices and experts in training. In small groups, newer colleagues might practice a skill with one another while the veterans work on a plan for when and where to implement the same skill within the existing curriculum.

> **Expert**
>
> Tailoring your training for new and experienced teachers provides a fun place to start thinking about differentiation. As you prepare, consider how you can set up activities that might separate and address the needs of these two participant types.

Nowadays, many people are familiar with the myths surrounding learning styles theories—the idea that people think and learn best in different modalities and that those styles affect retention (Biech, 2017; Garmston, 2018; Hattie, 2023; Saphier, 2017, Saphier et al., 2018; Willingham et al., 2015). That said, it's still best practice to craft and present training sessions so people might best access the information. So, instead of thinking of participants as adhering to one primary method of learning—visual, auditory, or kinesthetic—think of these ideas as learning *preferences*. For example, a person may prefer visual information but still process information auditorily and kinesthetically. Provide ways to access information aligned with the learning goal (Saphier et al., 2018; Willingham et al., 2015).

If a group needs to learn about circulating for safety in a lab setting, show a video of it, demonstrate it, and practice it. In short, make it both visual and kinesthetic. If the training involves a conceptual idea, such as understanding the concept of zero in number decomposition and place

> **Novice**
>
> Know that "standalone" or "one-shot" trainings are highly unlikely to change educator practice over time. Build in follow-up or other professional development designs around your training topic to ensure the workshop learning maintains a lasting impact.

value, then use manipulatives, illustrations, and research on mathematical misconceptions. Just as you coordinate your jacket or shoes to suit the weather outside, match the learning modality or style to the needs of the learning goal. Finally, consider pairs, small groups, whole groups, and solo work for both social interactions and reflection. Include reflection time that is chatty along with more quiet reflection time (Cain, 2013). Not everyone needs to talk to learn or reflect, yet some folks cannot think without verbalizing.

Understand the Limitations of Training

Providing training is not the only solution to educational problems. First off, training is not policy. If folks are well trained on a skill or an idea but return to a work environment systematically unsupportive of the new learning, then it's likely that minimal change in practice will occur. One-time, standalone training is not a solution for complex needs. Work to ensure classroom, school, and district policies and other structures promote the notions you are trying to convey through your training.

In addition, trainers in both business (Biech, 2017) and education (Joyce & Showers, 2002) found minimal work practice changed because of formal adult training only. Working adults tend to learn about 10 percent of what they know through traditional classes or training, 20 percent through social networking or by observing others, and about 70 percent through on-the-job demands—experimenting or practicing as part of a routine work assignment (Biech, 2017). People do not gain mastery of a skill or practice via training alone; there is simply not enough time. The very definition of "mastery" is the demonstration of a skill "consistently," "over time," and "in multiple settings" (Haring et al., 1978; Maki et al., 2022). Indeed, most educators become technically proficient through distributed practice in their job setting and with a great deal of feedback through coaching (Young et al., 2023).

To mitigate some of the limitations of a single workshop event, it is crucial to design adult professional development training that's part of a learning system with several different designs. We are big advocates of including prework and postwork or other follow-up activities to increase the likelihood that learning transfers back to the workplace; examples of both are provided in the next section. Also, look to Biech's *The Art and Science of Training* (2017), Easton's *Powerful Designs for Professional Learning* (2015), and the Association for Talent Development for exceptional sources for follow-up strategies. Over the years, we've collected or used several techniques to promote the transfer of workshop learning back to the worksite, and they are categorized here according to actions you might design to deploy before, during, or following training.

Before Training

- Send out a book, an article, or a white paper and request interaction with the material (e.g., answer a few questions, highlight three new ideas).
- Request completion of prerequisite elearning or virtual models. Is there an online module or practice that can be completed prior to the training?
- Send questions about the topic for participants to complete (Carpenter & Toftness, 2017; Watson & Busch, 2021).
- Recommend gathering and analyzing participants' work related to the training topic.
- Request joining a social network connected to the topic. Include response prompts participants can use to interact on the platform.

During Training

- Make action plans for implementation of workshop training.
- Role-play scenarios directly related to implementation in the work setting.
- Provide content that targets how-to information for the workplace setting.
- Ensure adequate practice during training. We found that overpracticing challenging skills provides participants with the confidence to apply the concept after training.
- Vigorously address participants' concerns about the implementation of training concepts. Anticipate potential roadblocks and plan

appropriate mitigation strategies in the agenda. Fully address participants' implementation concerns during training delivery.

- Have participants write a letter/postcard or an email to themselves about how they'll implement what they learned. Collect the self-addressed correspondence and, a few weeks later, mail the reminders to participants. For those who created an email, have them schedule the email to be sent a few weeks later.

After Training

- Participants work with small learning teams or professional learning communities by affinity, department, job, or cross-agency group (Easton, 2015; Little, 1993).
- Participants agree to be observed and provided with feedback by a mentor, a coach, or an outside expert (Joyce & Showers, 2002).
- Participants share work products with colleagues from other programs or agencies.
- Participants lead staff development or training sessions on the topic.
- Participants conduct microteaching sessions by demonstrating a small section of new learning for a colleague while that colleague provides feedback (Allen & Eve, 1968; Leong et al., 2021).
- Participants critique video examples of the new practices.
- In teams, participants conduct audits of student work, assignments, or test questions related to the training subject.
- Participants agree to engage in a study group about the topic.
- Participants keep a personal reflection log or journal about their progress implementing the training.
- Participants conduct action research on the subject in their work setting.
- Participants agree to use or create a job aide with the new information.
- Participants listen to training-related podcasts.
- Participants agree to solicit 360-degree evaluations (from peers, mentors, coaches, or administrators) specifically related to the training.

Virtual Training Tips for Training Design

All trainers must take into account not only physical training spaces but also virtual training spaces. The following are ideas to consider when designing training for the virtual environment:

- Choose online training platforms that enhance deep learning. Assure the platform provides the ability to communicate with participants before and after the training and offers interactive features for assessment of the learning (polls, quizzes, open-ended response, etc.) (Biggs et al., 2022).
- Use documents in a shared platform (e.g., Dropbox, Google Drive, Microsoft OneDrive, Slack) so participants maintain access before, during, and after training. Provide links to the files through the training platform chat, a shared folder, hyperlinks to shared documents, QR code links, or email (California Department of Education, 2023; Young & Dionne, 2020). Invariably, at least one person cannot access the documents in the manner you provide; anticipate this issue and share the documents in multiple formats.
- For small-group "report-out" time, use an app that lets participants create and format presentations and work with others in real time (e.g., Google Slides, Google Docs, Jamboard). As the presenter, use the links to monitor the in-training work completed by small teams.
- Incorporate asynchronous and synchronous work into the workshop. Before the group comes together, assign some required reading with a *specific task*, such as "Read the blog and copy and paste information you have questions about to this shared document. We will start the training by discussing what you added."
- Keep virtual workshops between two and four hours, with time for breaks. If the content calls for longer sessions, divide the content into smaller, more digestible chunks presented over multiple days.
- Try incorporating "spa" timeframes. In other words, end workshops 10 minutes before the hour. This premature ending allows participants to pause and interact with you (the trainer) and posit last-minute clarifications or questions.

- Send participants how-to information (tip sheets or links) on managing the online platform in advance. Try to get basic technology needs addressed beforehand so the training time is pertinent to content and not focused on how to use the technology.
- Plan to use dual monitors; this makes managing documents, participant videos, and screen shares easier.
- Expect to cover less content in online settings than during in-person training.
- Plan physical minibreaks during longer sessions. Have participants stand up and touch four walls or take part in chair yoga. Encourage participants to help you lead these stretch breaks.
- Allow for awkward silence. Uncomfortable breaks in conversation during virtual training can be challenging. However, it is vital to allow wait time (Rowe, 1986). After you ask a question to a virtual group, wait 10–15 seconds for someone to respond in the chat or find the unmute button and speak. Clearly state your intention to pause for responses.
- Construct group norms specific to the virtual environment (Aguilar, 2016; Mroz et al., 2018; Smutny, 2019), such as muting background noise, participating in the chat, showing video, engaging in small-group work, and avoiding multitasking (Ophir et al., 2009; Parry & Le Roux, 2021).
- Reduce the number of programs or platforms you use, especially if virtual training is new to you or making you anxious. Multiple programs and platforms exist for virtual training; it can be overwhelming to determine which ones best align with a virtual environment. Young and Dionne (2020) offer the following criteria to evaluate which integration to use:
    — Does this program check participants' understanding of the content?
    — Does this program help participants create a presentation?
    — Does this program gamify the training?
    — Will this program help people search for information?
    — Can this program facilitate the sharing of information among participants and between the trainer and participants?
    — Will this program help participants apply the training information?

- Reduce the number of managed files to help reduce the amount of toggling between multiple documents that's required. Both a slide deck and PDF handouts are often unnecessary; combine all training content into one format or the other.
- Provide how-to sheets or a miniworkshop (in advance of the primary workshop) on using the virtual platform if participants are new to the program.
- Post a video introduction of yourself to accelerate team building and reduce time spent in introductions (virtually or in person). Invite participants with a link in advance, and ask them to post video introductions of themselves (Silberman et al., 2015).

2

Training Delivery

Training delivery provides guidance for trainers' decisions made "in the moment" of presenting. This chapter helps the trainer complete the following:

- Facilitate robust, equitable discussions (Lemov, 2021; Silberman et al., 2015) and field questions (Hattie & Clarke, 2019; Saphier et al., 2018).
- Provide clear directions (Garmston, 2018; Lemov, 2021; Saphier et al., 2018).
- Establish trust and rapport (Aguilar, 2013, 2016; Bloom et al., 2005; Noddings, 2013; Saphier et al., 2018).
- Promote care (Noddings, 2013).
- Communicate appropriate body language (Hattie, 2023; Van Edward, 2017).
- Manage nerves (Bicch, 2017; Damisch et al., 2010).

Ways to implement some of these ideas in the virtual environment appear at the end of the chapter. Target your area of training needs and try out the strategies we've gathered; think of them like souvenirs from hundreds of powerful trainers.

Facilitate Robust, Equitable Discussions

Facilitating discussions proves to be one of the most exciting yet potentially challenging aspects of training. The following methods provide a framework compiled from tips gathered from virtuoso trainers from around the world—trainers who deployed various tactics to make group discussions a learning experience for everyone involved. Moreover, several authors informed this section, including Lemov (2021) and Silberman and colleagues (2015).

Anchor the Discussion

Maintain a clear intent, rationale, or goal for the discussion. When planning training, ask yourself, "What do I want *every* person in the room to gain from this whole-group exchange?" Write out the question for your group and note *why* you're asking it. The following list includes a few potential purposes for a group discussion:

- Share general ideas.
- Decide as a group.
- Describe something learned.
- List recommendations for a decision-maker.
- Define an abstract concept.
- Brainstorm solutions to a specific problem.
- Analyze a pattern.
- Generate ideas.
- Air concerns.
- Evaluate progress.
- Celebrate success.

Glance back at Figure 1.2 (p. 17) to see if you're soliciting the type and level of thinking you want from the group. You may need to redraft the question after you've reviewed the purpose and DoK level you want to elicit. Draft a couple of backup questions (that narrow the scope of your initial inquiry) in case there are few or no responses to the first question. For example, if "What did you notice about the two video examples?" solicits no response, then try to be more precise: "What did students say in the first video that they didn't say in the second one? Why was that?"

Now list potential responses you hope to raise. Writing such a list may help you rewrite your original whole-group question. During training, use the list of potential responses as a personal checklist to keep the conversation focused on your goal. If the discussion goes off topic, use your "rationale for the discussion" to bring the group talk back to your purpose. For example, say, "I hear everyone trying to solve Silvio's problem right now. We can do that for Silvio during teamwork after the break. *For now,* let's keep the discussion more general; what ideas does the group have for *any person* facing this issue?" Finally, if participants do not reach the epiphanies you want from your initial and backup questions, simply tell them what you want them to understand before closing the discussion. This is where your clear (and written) intent for the discussion comes in handy—just state what you wrote.

Novice

Many highly skilled trainers recommend listing potential participant responses to key workshop questions. It is a great way to anticipate comments and link participants' insights to the learning goals. In some cases, it may also help you manage challenging comments. If you write out responses for counterarguments or common misconceptions regarding your topic, then you're more likely to remain calm and provide clearer responses when you encounter pushback or disagreement from participants.

Expand the Discussion

At times, it can be challenging to promote a robust group conversation; when this occurs, connect an individual's comments to the training goals or another person's statement. Alternatively, try asking more open-ended or divergent questions—*why* and *how* queries—instead of questions that require only a single word or phrase. For more help with open-ended questions, plan DoK 3 prompts (see Chapter 1). Occasionally, probe individuals with phrases such as "Tell us more" or "Can you give an example?" Finally, consider utilizing wait time, which simply means pausing for 5–10 seconds between asking a question and calling on someone or making another comment—and waiting 5–10 seconds after a person responds before you comment (Rowe, 1986; Saphier et al., 2018). A well-researched approach, wait time allows for more extended discussion and higher levels of thinking during group talk, but it does take discipline and practice to acquire and use well.

Novice

If you struggle to use wait time, try putting reminder notes on your training materials, computer, or podium. Alternatively, have a friend or coach track your wait time during workshops and provide you with feedback during breaks and after training.

Clarify the Discussion

Paraphrase and summarize when someone speaks at length or when you can't follow their train of thought. If you don't understand what someone said, odds are that others in the group also don't understand. Likewise, listen for vague or generalized terms and acronyms and press for specificity as needed. When participants use definitive phrases such as *all students, none of the parents,* or *they won't let us,* gently and sincerely push back, asking, "How many students precisely?" "Which parents?" or "Who said that?" Finally, revisit the rationale or original question for the discussion, if needed. Simply repeating the purpose might help folks clarify their comments. These tactics allow the speaker—and those listening to them—to be more specific in their thinking.

Manage Highly Verbal Participants

A couple of issues may be the case if one person verbally commandeers discussions. First, you might need to rethink your design and include more small-group and partner activities. More intimate interactions provide some folks with the verbal processing time and confidence they need to contribute to whole-group discussions. See if that remedies the situation. If needed, pause a whole-group discussion and ask people to talk with a partner for a few minutes. Then restart the whole-group discussion to see if you generate more comments from a larger variety of participants.

Second, you might need to remind the group of the training norms if agreements exist about sharing the discussion or equitable talk. Sometimes, you may even need to jump into their comments: "Let me gently interrupt you. Let's hear from someone else about *why* what you said might be true." Alternatively, "That's a valid point. I'm going to ask you to hit the pause button for a moment while we hear from someone with a counterargument." If necessary, speak to the participant individually during a break in training, remind them of the group agreements, and ask them to allow others more airtime. A workshop leader who doesn't manage a verbally domineering participant proves to be one of the main hindrances to other participants' engagement (Mroz et al., 2018; Odermatt et al., 2018). If the person is a big talker *and* a challenging participant, check out more approaches to managing that situation in Chapter 4.

Novice

If you're nervous about confronting a talkative participant, simply try interrupting them with something like, "OK, give me just a second. Let's do a quick partner talk for three minutes. Then we'll come back to the whole-group discussion." This tiny break may mitigate their need to control the whole group, moving forward. It may also give you a few seconds to think of other strategies to use if they continue the undesired behavior.

Manage Nonverbal Participants

We led training sessions for years before we realized what we thought was a highly thoughtful discussion was really only a chat between the trainer and two or three other people—not all or even most of the participants. However, expert trainers all tend to have one thing in common:

They work hard to get *everyone* engaged during whole-group discussions. This practice finds support in research that shows employees feel more engaged when teams are fully participatory (Allen & Rogelberg, 2013) and in studies of cultural sensitivity that show most populations prefer participative leadership (Chhokar et al., 2019; House et al., 2014). Furthermore, when leaders pay attention to interactional fairness in groups, attendees prove more likely to participate (Kauffeld & Lehmann-Willenbrock, 2012; Mroz et al., 2018). The following paragraphs offer suggestions for promoting more equitable participation in group discussions.

Who isn't talking? One of the swiftest ways to check the number of people responding is to note who is *not* talking. Pay special attention to women and people of color, since they may be talked over, interrupted, or excluded. Redirect the discussion to those participants who are being undermined: "Let's hear from someone who hasn't shared with the whole group." Keep an eye out for body language signs. Are people covering their mouths or holding their throats? It might mean they want to speak (Van Edward, 2017).

As mentioned previously with the "highly verbal participant," remind the group of the group's norms, particularly if you posted and explained expectations for participation at the beginning of the workshop. Say, "Let me gently remind myself and the group that we have a norm of allowing everyone a chance to speak. Let's check ourselves and make sure that's happening." Alternatively, try, "OK, I want to pause the whole group. In your small teams, take a moment to whip around the group and tell one another how you're doing with promoting our norm 'Everyone gets airtime.' Give yourself a self-rating. Go!" Often, adults self-correct their behavior when provided with a good-natured reminder.

You can always try a general reminder: "Who needs to speak who hasn't shared yet?" Better yet, be more direct: "I glance around the room and see lots of folks covering their mouths. Is there something others need to contribute?" If participants remain quiet, switch gears. Think of a way to immerse everyone in the topic through a brief small-group discussion, writing activity, group alert (Kounin & Sherman, 1979), or polling activity. Then relaunch the whole-group discussion.

> **Expert** Up your game by planning tactics to gain discussion from all or nearly all participants. Track who's talking and who's not. At a minimum, never be satisfied with only a few folks doing all the talking. Target an 80 percent engagement rate. Then try to get 90 percent or more involved.

Wrap Up the Discussion

In general, keep track of how long talks about specific topics typically take. Once you notice patterns, adjust future training plans, reducing or adding time as needed. If you must end the discussion (for time or other reasons), say something like "I *love* this discussion. At the same time, I'm going to gently [or respectfully] move us on to the next topic" or "OK, let's hit the pause button on this topic. We'll revisit this topic when we talk about ____ later in training."

If tensions are high, people seem emotional, or an irreconcilable issue arises during the discussion—but you *must* move forward—try an acknowledgment tactic. Acknowledging is remarking aloud that you understand people's feelings or the situation. This is a powerful and straightforward approach for managing affective needs (Aguilar 2013, 2016; Saphier et al., 2018). Try this. Say, "I'm fully aware many of us have strong emotions remaining around this issue. *(pause)* That said, I need to bring this topic to a close for now." Alternatively, conduct a lengthier version of acknowledgment by saying, "Grab some paper and write everything you're thinking or feeling about the issue at this moment. I'll give you three minutes to write. *(pause for the writing)* Now, what you wrote is important, and we cannot address it further right now. Fold it nicely and put it away. We're moving forward to our next section of training."

> **Expert** If the topic is sensitive or controversial and you need to move on, keep in mind that some people may have strong feelings but are not verbally complaining, so pay attention to body language. Scan the room. If

Expert
(continued)

you're seeing lots of folded arms, little or no eye contact, folks covering their mouths or throats, or people slumped over or turned away
from you, it *may* mean they're thinking something they are not saying
(Hattie & Clark, 2019; Van Edward, 2017). At this point, do an acknowledging strategy with writing even though participants are not saying much.
Some people vent or emote in writing before they do so verbally. Whether
they're upset or not, you've provided a moment for them to articulate
their concerns before transitioning to the next workshop activity.

Conduct an Equitable Group "Report Out"

One of the quickest ways to pummel participant engagement during
training is by *overrelying* on one participant to speak while the rest of the
group sits and watches. This "sitting in silence" typically happens when
the trainer calls on one person from each small group to "report out" what
occurred during teamwork. To avoid this lack of full-group participation,
evaluate the workshop design by asking yourself if it's necessary to hear a
representative from every small group; most times, it isn't. Perhaps only
two or three examples need to be heard by the whole group (which is our
personal rule of thumb). This section offers a few alternatives to "one person reporting out."

Instead of waiting for the end of small-group work to hear what each
team completed, try fishing for appropriate information during the small-
group work time. During this time, circulate among the groups and

- Find a couple of teams to share their stellar findings or epiphanies.
  Then ask only those two teams to share their work with the entire
  group when it is time for the work teams to report back to the
  whole group.
- Note errors and perhaps reteach what needs correcting with the
  entire group. Then, when it's time for the work teams to report
  back to the whole group, instead of having folks report out, simply
  reteach the whole group based on the errors you surfaced during
  small-group work.

- Find a model response or product from among the groups and share it with the whole group. If you circulate among the work teams and find an exemplar you want the entire group to see, then when whole-group time occurs, share the model instead of asking to hear from each small group.

Another option involves having small groups contribute their work to a shared drive that everyone in the training accesses and reviews without subjecting them all to sitting and listening to a few people verbally and laboriously describe what they did with their team.

Novice

Seriously reconsider verbal reports from every group following small-group work. Typically, you only need to hear from two or three teams, not all of them.

If you must call on one participant to respond while the whole group is sitting and listening, use a group alert (Kounin & Sherman, 1979; WestEd, 2016). Provide an explicit, observable action for people to perform as they listen. For example, say, "Listen to Monica's answer. As she talks, jot down what she says"; "Write down any of the key terms you hear LeVar use"; "Listen to Judith's answer. If you have the same answer, circle it. If you wrote something else, write down what Judith says"; "If you agree with Fernando's reply, I want to hear loud finger snaps of agreement." Key here is that you circulated beforehand and know that all these responses are the "answers" everyone needs to hear.

Many people who volunteer to speak are the quickest thinkers, the loudest speakers, or the most assertive individuals. People who have been marginalized or are accustomed to being dismissed may not speak up. Therefore, providing whole-group response techniques such as a group alert offers one way to get their opinion (via finger snaps) or participation (via writing) into the workshop more equitably. To promote even more equity in training, check out the total-group participation tactics in Chapter 3.

Expert

The group alert is the hallmark of an expert trainer. Rarely do we see a highly proficient workshop leader who is not a champion of this approach.

Field Questions

The first rule of fielding questions involves knowing your training content exceptionally well. Know what you know, know what you don't know, and keep handy resources for accessing further information if participants need it. If your training materials contain frequently asked questions (FAQs), memorize them; they're called "frequently asked" for a reason. Learn the FAQs by heart—just as you would a second language or colleagues' names.

Once you thoroughly understand your topic, practice a few techniques for managing unexpected questions and supplying diplomatic responses during training. Selecting among the following possible responses proves easier if you maintain a clear goal or intent:

- Summarize the question if it is long or if you are unclear about the intention or details of the question.
- If the question is not directly related to the training content, ask the person to write down the request and hand it to you. Let them know you'll get them an answer later. If the issue is significant to them, they'll take the time to bring you the information.
- Use wait time. Wait 5–10 seconds after a question (or comment) before you respond. While you wait, the person may restate their original question or comment with more precision. Moreover, another participant may respond to the person speaking with a better retort than yours. There are multiple benefits to using wait time.
- Toss the question back to the group. Say, "I have an idea, but I'd like to hear what the group thinks first." Use this approach when there are multiple correct responses to the question. If there exists a single, simple, correct answer, answer the question yourself.

- Offer to speak to the person during a break or at the end of training. Use this maneuver when you think the response is not generalizable for the whole group. Some people ask for help so narrow in scope that the issue cannot be addressed appropriately in training; they might need a one-on-one consult. If you can help them, move your assistance to an individual setting.
- Correct misinformation *when there is only one correct response.* As adults learn new material, it is essential to ensure the information in the training room is accurate. This practice applies the principle of learning "knowledge of results" or feedback (Hattie & Clarke, 2019; Saphier et al., 2018). Try these responses:
  - Simply correct the speaker: "The correct answer is *implicit*, not *explicit*" or (with a genuine smile) "No, the correct answer is _____."
  - Encourage the speaker: (*with a smile*) "That's not quite it; try again."
  - Correct the speaker and ask them to explain the correction: "No, that is not what we needed; _____ is the right response. Can you explain why that's not an example of _____?"
  - Point out the part of the speaker's response that is correct: "You had the first part right. The correct answer is _____."
  - Supply the correct information for the speaker's incorrect response: "Your answer is an example of a *microaggression. Systemic racism* is the correct answer for this example."
  - Use positive intent: "What you said isn't correct, but I'm glad you mentioned it because other people in the room are likely to think that, too." This approach is addressed more thoroughly in Chapter 4 (Bailey, 2011, 2015; Costa et al., 2016; Patterson et al., 2021).
- Make openness to critical feedback a group norm or expectation. Everyone is learning, and everyone may struggle with the content. Keep in mind that, for the most part, adults are open to making mistakes; they won't be devastated by being corrected (Fishbach & Finkelstein, 2020; Fong et al., 2018; Killion, 2019; Zenger & Folkman, 2014).
- When someone responds incorrectly—and *there are multiple correct responses*—or your goal is to keep people open and thinking,

use one of the following prompts. This approach works well when the training design uses constructed knowledge and you're working on getting the group to understand a concept before explicitly defining it.

— Cue the speaker, giving minimal (but further) guidance to the correct response: "You have the basic data from the study correct. How did the discussion in the same study explain the findings?"

— Repeat the question several times as needed.

— Ask the speaker if they need more time or assistance from you or another participant.

— Ask the speaker to support their answer with some data or an example.

— Challenge the speaker: "Convince the room you're correct."

— Respond with gentle guidance: "Go back and check your text to see if it supports your answer."

— Introduce a counterargument or neglected information if you're not hearing the necessary information: "How would you explain that idea to a skeptic?"

Novice

Novice trainers often struggle with incorrect responses from adults and simply nod or ignore the inaccurate information. Practice saying aloud three or four of these responses to incorrect answers; think of it like conducting a tiny "dress rehearsal" of correcting misinformation before training.

Expert

Memorize a few of these progressive minimal cues. Particularly with constructed knowledge activities, highly skilled trainers sometimes rush to supply the correct response without providing participants with ample productive struggle time.

- Consider the following tactics when you field questions from participants you perceive as challenging:

    — Assume positive intent, and pretend there is a friendly rationale behind the question: "Oh! I'm glad to answer your question; it gives me another chance to explain my earlier point. I think I can explain it more fully this time." In this example, your positive intent is the diplomatic assumption the person is helping make the training clearer. For more details about positive intent, see Chapter 4.

    — Tie the comments to the training objective, and make the speaker your "training helper": "You're bringing up a point we'll address this afternoon. Thanks for helping me preview the info."

    — Dignify or simply state differences, especially with philosophical differences: "That's a different approach than what I'm advocating here."

    — Avoid prolonged discussions about abstractions unless it is the training subject: "That's a different school of thought, and we're not working on that in today's training."

    — Offer a different example or analogy.

    — Recognize and acknowledge expertise: "You understand your children better than anyone else in this training."

    — Attempt "feel-felt-found" (Garmston, 2018; Gordon & Burch, 2010): "You *say* you feel ____. I felt similarly when ____. What I found was ____."

    — Sincerely offer an "I don't want; I do want" alternative (Patterson et al., 2021): "I don't want you to think ____. I do want you to think ____."

Novice

Positive intent stands out as the go-to tactic of highly proficient trainers. Memorize this approach, practice it repeatedly, and use it liberally. Positive intent helps mitigate numerous challenging situations and typically elicits more effective communication with a variety of participants. See Chapter 4 for more details about positive intent.

Expert

We notice that most skilled trainers frequently manage discussions about off-topic philosophies with the simple approach of dignifying differences.

Novice

Both "feel-felt-found" and "I don't want; I do want" are acknowledging moves made by the trainer. The advantage of using one of these frames is that you provide a more thorough, more explicit recognition or acknowledgment to the person. For this reason, both scripts are supported in the research as effective communication strategies.

Provide Clear Directions

For years, we led a train-the-trainer program and noticed a pattern among struggling presenters: Their group directions created confusion because they only provided vague guidance. Trainers might interrupt instructions to tell a quick story, causing people to forget the steps communicated before the anecdote. Disarray occurs when guidelines are supplied out of order. The following sections include our seven attributes of successful directions.

Get People's Attention

It is essential to connect with everyone's eyes and ears before providing directions. This helps reduce the need for repetition and helps those trying to listen to you be unhindered by distracting side conversations. If the group is small, a flashy signal is unnecessary. Huge groups, however, may need an obtrusive interruption to grab everyone's attention. Here are several ideas to signal "All quiet now!" Whatever approach you use, try to use it consistently:

- Turn the lights on and off.
- Start or stop background music.
- Sound a chime, timer, or instrument.
- Start a simple clapping rhythm, chant, cheer, or song.

- Ask participants to stand and stretch when they finish a task. As the last person stands, deliver the next steps.

Tell people your signaling narrative. For example, say, "This is my signal to listen. I'll say, 'Finish up your conversation.' I'll wait half a minute. Then I'll say, 'Give me your attention, please.'" Explain this from the beginning of the workshop and repeat it throughout, and you'll find that it works efficiently.

Early in one seminar, we watched an experienced trainer lift a colossal antique school bell and provide a brief, touching story about their late grandmother who once taught in a one-room, rural Missouri schoolhouse. The trainer held their grandma's actual school bell and said the bell was the signal to stop and listen. In one fell swoop, the trainer made a personal connection and hooked participants' attention. The room screeched to silence every time the bell rang out.

Describe What to Do

High-quality directions focus participants on *what to do*—not on *what not to do* (Lemov, 2021; Watson & Busch, 2021; Wegner et al., 1987). For example, clearly and succinctly say, "Open the folder and take out the thick handout. Then hold up the handout." Avoid rambling on and on: "Don't go into your binder; get the manipulatives instead. Ignore the highlighters for now, and don't worry about the photo examples right now. Find the purple handout."

The second example focuses participants on extraneous issues they don't need to know and ultimately sows more discord than guidance. Primary teachers are familiar with a hard and fast rule: It's far more effective to call out, "Walking!" than it is to say, "Stop running!" In short, when delivering directions, the effective elementary school teacher and the powerful presenter focus on *what to do*.

Expert

On the few occasions we witness experienced trainers trip up with directions, it typically involves describing what to do or being sequential. Pay attention to these components so you can be fully proficient with explicit directions.

Be Sequential

Provide no more than three or four consecutive steps at a time (Cowan, 2000), making sure you stop to see that all steps are completed. For example, if there are 10 or 12 procedures to complete, give only three or four steps at a time until the instructions finish. If a genuinely colossal mess occurs in the middle of directions and everyone ends up in the wrong place, use a signal, get everyone's attention, and restart the directions. Don't yell over the group to correct steps as they complete a task; this provides an inappropriate model of talking over others, and several people will not be able to hear your instructions over the noise.

Use a Microphone

When in doubt, use a microphone. People cannot hear you in a large room, no matter how strong you think your voice is. Just use the mic.

Make Them Show You

Tell participants to do something easily observable or actionable. Instead of saying something elusive like "Find the photograph in your handout packet," try "Get the paper calendar and hold it up so I can see it." Don't say, "Fill in the workbook"; rather, announce, "Once you finish writing answers on page 14 of the workbook, stand up so I can see that you have finished." A quick visual scan of the crowd lets you know if folks are with you or not. There's no need to ask, "Did everyone understand?"

Stand Still for Directions

Walk around the room while presenting, delivering information, telling a story, or engaging with participants during small-group work. By contrast, stand still when you provide directions. Select one spot in the room from which you will deliver all instructions. One trainer referred to this tactic as "park and bark"—you park yourself in one spot and bark the directions. The technique offers a subtle cue for the group to pay attention when they see you in this spot (Garmston, 2018; Lemov, 2021). It also increases workshop pacing by reducing the time spent rallying everyone's attention.

Announce the Ending

When a pilot announces that the plane is preparing for its final descent or when a waiter lets you know they'll return with the check, they provide a space of readiness for what comes next. Likewise, when the end of a workshop activity is imminent, give participants a heads-up so they can complete the task as scheduled. This tactic allows participants to disengage physically and affectively from activities (Saphier et al., 2018). It also increases the likelihood that people are ready to focus on the next set of directions. Furthermore, studies have revealed that telling people how much time they have for a task increases activity engagement, motivation, and performance (Katzir et al., 2020). Remind the group to complete the current activity in 2, 5, or 10 minutes, or post a timer on the training screen.

Novice

Explicit directions occur second only to participant engagement in terms of what we most frequently coach new trainers on. There is a difference between delivering directions to a class of students and commanding a room of 60–100 adults in terms of effectively delivering instructions. We strongly recommend you write out directions for training, word for word, the first six or seven times you train. Then ask a colleague to use the seven components listed here to provide you with feedback on your directions.

Establish Trust and Rapport

A modicum of camaraderie between the trainer and attendees helps facilitate robust learning during a workshop; this occurs by focusing on trust and rapport. Providing both a challenging and a comfortable environment sets an ideal climate for learning and addresses a primary principle of learning—feeling tone (Saphier et al., 2018). Our experience, along with several authors' and researchers' findings (Aguilar, 2013, 2016; Bloom et al., 2005; Noddings, 2013), has revealed practical ways to create predictable and stimulating training conditions without relying on trainer charisma. You can be a diplomatic trainer without attempting to be every participant's best friend.

- Focus on common work goals. Let people know you are working on improving work conditions and outcomes. Be specific and connect workshop goals to participants' everyday job goals.
- Be genuinely interested in participants' implementation of the training goals. Make connections to everyday work tasks.
- Tell stories or analogies that communicate your expertise with the subject.
- Keep your commitment to start and end on time, and remember to answer questions you sidelined for later.

Novice

Highly effective trainers do not need to be charismatic personalities or educational entertainers. You do not need to be best friends with everyone you train. However, you do need some basic skills of trust, rapport, and care in order to establish genuine, professional relations with others. Doing this helps you be a stronger communicator, and it helps participants learn more effectively from your workshop.

Promote Care

It is challenging to care for people we don't know very well or who do something we don't like. Training workshops, though, offer the perfect time to practice what education philosopher Nel Noddings (2013) calls ethical care—the kind of care demonstrated for others because it is our obligation or part of the job to care for them. To imagine this concept, think of the practice of care shown by social workers and nurses. Now imagine your trusted doctor, mechanic, accountant, or pet sitter—someone you know but who's not a close friend or relative. What do they do to communicate care to you? Think carefully about their actions; you may discover that they demonstrate some of the same skills and employ some of the same tactics we recommend you try in training. The following list provides discrete, actionable tactics for telegraphing care to training participants.

Model Care

- Pay attention to details about your environment; keep it clean and clear of clutter.
- Make materials professional and tidy; align the graphic design to the learning goal of the workshop.
- Practice manners; say "please" and "thank you."
- Show genuine appreciation and offer appropriate feedback for what you hear and see.
- Summarize participants' comments if necessary.
- Make connections to everyday work or training goals. Be curious about participants' perspectives on the workshop subject and their jobs.
- Give people airtime away from the group, letting them know they can work with you during breaks. After a rough encounter with someone during training, revisit your conversation during a break or small-group work; reach out to show that you are unafraid of difficult discussions and want to check for further clarification or understanding. There is no need to agree or provide solutions; it's simply important to work to comprehend their perspective and be able to contrast their understanding with yours.
- Be quick to apologize when you make mistakes.

Encourage Care Among Participants

- Make sure feedback loops are positive and focus on data, not just feelings or unsupported claims.
- Clarify an expectation to help one another if participants don't understand something or need assistance with work products.

Recognize That Gratitude Goes a Long Way

- Publicly thank people for helping one another. For participants who go out of their way to demonstrate service to the group or another individual, offer a public cheer or prize. Indeed, gratitude goes a long way (Emmons, 2016).
- Make sure participants thank their partners after pair or small-group work.
- Even when there is no evidence of care, praise the approximation of care. For example, if people are not making positive comments in their feedback to partners, say, "I see people are thinking carefully about the positive comment you want to include" or "I know everyone is ready to tack on positive remarks at the end of your feedback." This response praises the expected action, even if there's a lack of evidence for it.

Practice Positive Intent

- Assume the best possible reason behind the behavior you witness. To help with this concept, try to assume that, in most cases, people are attempting to care for their personal needs to be heard, respected, or acknowledged.
- Mirror the behavior you want to see from participants. Be ready with strategies for behaviors that push your buttons, and deliver those tactics graciously and calmly. Trainers who demonstrate calm and politeness in the face of anger and rudeness typically arrive at a peaceful resolution. Most people just don't have the energy to sustain ill will for an extended period of time when they don't get the expected response.

Engage in Dialogue

Try to listen and try to be heard. Listen carefully to the question, the terminology used, and the intent for the question. Make your point another way if your explanation is not helping to explain a concept.

Communicate Appropriate Body Language

Nonverbal physical cues often provide the trainer with hints of participants' understanding—or lack thereof. Open and forward-leaning gestures—raised eyebrows, extended eye contact, open palms, nodding head—*may* indicate people are actively accepting the message they're hearing; the group is with you. By contrast, people with folded arms, crossed legs, and bodies turned away from you *might* signal that they disagree with or don't want to be part of the topic at hand; consider these gestures "closed and back" body language. Remember, these indicators are often oversimplified; body language can be applied and understood differently in different situational and cultural contexts.

It's important not to overgeneralize body language, but you should still use it as one of several indicators of participants' receptivity to learning—and in a few different ways. First, check in with participants if you're seeing a lot of closed indicators (from either an individual or a group). Ask, "How's the training going for you? How are you taking in the information?" Give folks a chance to explain. It's possible someone might reveal that what you've interpreted as closed gestures are actually because they're in physical pain from a backache. Second, ensure you use open body language yourself as much as possible. You want to show participants you are receptive to their ideas, enjoy the topic, and are comfortable with the group. For more in-depth information about body language or to improve your communication skills, check Van Edward's excellent *Captivate: The Science of Succeeding with People* (2017).

Manage Your Nerves

We worked with many trainers who maintain significant nervousness regarding training. Somewhat ironically, trainers who report feeling nervous recommend being *overprepared* as the best remedy. Use that nervous energy to practice your demonstration, give directions, or ask questions—20 times each. Use a timer and practice chunks of the training out loud. Script what you'll say and do and what participants might say in response. If possible, visit the training site the day before, set out all the supplies, and conduct a rehearsal (Biech, 2017). Visualize yourself in front of the room, calm and confident. Even seasoned pros do this; we've watched comedian Wanda Sykes walk through a comedy routine in an empty auditorium, telling jokes and pausing to comment, "Big laughs here. Big laughs here!"

Explore the idea of scripting out the training if you're particularly anxious. For one idea about how to accomplish this, see Figure 3.1 (p. 71) where we share an approach for noting the trainer's and participants' actions during each training section.

Several trainers tell us they carry an amulet, a tiny personal object reminding them who they are outside training. This object, perhaps a framed photo of a child or a cherished miniature figurine set near the podium, provides a small visual anchor of calm in the sometimes turbulent waves of a workshop. The research even supports this practice. Researchers determined that individuals who carried "lucky charms" improved their performance in motor and cognitive tasks as well as their self-efficacy (Damisch et al., 2010). In training, Tamarra uses a Superman bag to remind her of her husband (who is nicknamed Superman), and Keith carries a poker chip gifted to him by a veteran trainer after a weeklong training decades ago: "See that Vera Bradley bag over there? It's full of knitting and two novels; it's my workshop bag, so I have something worthwhile to do during training, and I didn't touch it this week. I give away poker chips for outstanding work; here's yours for your training this week." The chip rests affectionately in Keith's presenter kit, as an amulet, to this day.

Virtual Training Tips for Training Delivery

- Provide information in advance about the expectations of the session. Do participants join from their own device? Can they turn on the camera while in a room with friends? Is it expected for the group to have their cameras on the entire session? Is there an article to read beforehand so conversation can happen immediately? Prepare a single landing page or dashboard for the session's pertinent logistical details (date, time, meeting link, contact information, homework, links to articles or videos).

- Before or during training, provide basic technical guidelines or norms for the virtual environment. For example, reminders to disable pop-ups, mute when not talking, turn off email or text notifications, and set up an out-of-office auto-response.
- Gently nudge when participation is lacking: "I see four participants responded in the chat. We have 30 more seconds while everyone responds."
- While participants are in breakout rooms, visit or roam the rooms to listen to conversations. This is an opportune time to "tap" participants so they are prepared to respond when returning to the main group. Say, "What a unique perspective! Do you mind sharing that when we are all together in the larger group?"
- Provide an electronic warning that time is coming to an end before closing breakout rooms. This tactic is referred to as providing notice; it gives people a couple of minutes to mentally and emotionally detach from the small group (Saphier et al., 2018). When possible, reveal a timer on your screen during timed activities.
- If the virtual platform does not have a built-in option, use an application that allows all questions to be tracked and held in one place for reference during and after training.
- Use open body language to communicate virtually. Slightly lean into the camera using open hand gestures, smiling, and raising your eyebrows.
- The act of "punching" or accentuating essential terms is done verbally with in-person training. Consider turning off your screen for a dramatic effect whenever a point needs emphasis in online work. Do this by stopping the screen share and speaking directly into the camera. Often unexpected, participants may think something went wrong with the presentation or their computer. Say, "I stopped sharing on purpose; this next point is important."
- Conduct a rehearsal with family members or colleagues if this is your first virtual meeting. Managing the logistics of online training

along with the content can be overwhelming. A dry run helps iron out the kinks, particularly with activity directions. Set up some mistakes to manage, such as people not accessing materials in advance, trouble with breakout rooms, or audio glitches (Lemov et al., 2012; Zoom, 2022). At a minimum, rehearse the opening of the session so the start is smooth.

- For complex individual and small-group tasks, include no more than four explicit steps and place the directions directly in the print materials. Go further and copy those instructions into the chat as you review them or provide a QR code link to the directions. This process may reduce downtime spent reexplaining directions.

- Let people know in advance how you expect them to take notes during virtual training. Will they have a booklet or handout they can print beforehand, or will all materials be electronic versions? We suggest more options rather than fewer; this way, people can accommodate their needs. For example, some folks prefer paper and do not mind the time or expense involved in printing materials; give them the option to print.

- Consider using a second screen that provides you, the trainer, with a view that mirrors the participants' view. Use your primary screen for presenting and your second screen for monitoring what participants see; this helps you note issues with covered documents or faulty video views and make corrections more quickly. In place of a second screen, you could use a tablet or phone to monitor the participants' view. We've even noticed some presenters borrow a tip from online gamers and install a third screen, mount it vertically instead of horizontally, and use it solely to monitor the group chat.

3

Engaging Participants

There are lots of ways to learn. People acquire knowledge by watching a movie or video, listening to a speech, hearing a podcast or conversation, sitting in a lecture, pondering personal thoughts, browsing a social media post, or reading a novel. Nevertheless, a vast body of research asserts that we learn more and retain that learning longer when our *interaction* with the information increases (Archer & Hughes, 2011; Biech, 2017; Biggs et al., 2022; Darling-Hammond et al., 2020; NASEM, 2018; Saphier et al., 2018; Wammes et al., 2019). Additionally, a meta-analysis of research revealed staff satisfaction improved with participatory meetings (Mroz et al., 2018). Our experience indicates active participation proves to be one of the most salient principles of learning that workshop leaders deploy to increase the rate and retention of learning. Moreover, engaging attendees breathes life and energy into training. Training with minimal participant involvement becomes a bit like a long walk in tight shoes: exhausting and regrettable.

Participant engagement proves paramount to effective training, and this chapter supplies numerous methods, organized into seven broad categories, for promoting involvement in workshop learning: writing, speaking, reading, signaling, drawing, listening or watching, and demonstrating. Most tactics produce observable actions the trainer can monitor to quickly ascertain the degree of participation or learning. A few strategies here generate more elusive processes that surreptitiously engross adults in the training content. As several researchers suggest (Archer & Hughes, 2011; Himmele & Himmele, 2017; Saphier et al., 2018), we prefer these engagement activities completed in unison so everyone responds simultaneously and reveals their responses together. Use the lists in the following sections to select a variety of engagement strategies that are harmonized to your training style, the needs of your participants, and your workshop goals.

Write

Simultaneous writing provides one of the quickest ways to engage adult participants in training. Writing inserts time to think and articulate. In fact, some people are not even certain what they think about some topics until they've had a minute or two to ponder it; writing offers that moment. Less verbal participants may appreciate the occasional workshop activity that does not require talking with others. The other beauty of writing activities is they may be tailored to training time constraints. If you're short on time, do a one-word response on blank paper flashed to the trainer. If you need to fill more time, ask folks to complete a one-minute paper or write out a counterargument.

1. **5-3-1:** Participants write five essential points, three new ideas, and one question they have about the training's reading, demonstration, or discussion.
2. **Minute Paper:** Participants write for 60 seconds about the presentation and respond to the questions "What do I want to know today?" "What are the five important points to remember so far?" and "What is left unanswered from today's work?"

3. **Argument, Counterargument:** Participants fold a piece of paper in half. On one side, they write the advantages of an idea or position. On the opposite side, they write a counterpoint to the argument.

4. **Bookmark:** Provide participants with a blank bookmark. Have them add crucial points and ideas. (Use a note card or sticky note with the same intent.)

5. **Caption:** Participants take pictures of a slide, an article, or a work product from the presentation. They summarize learning by writing captions that describe details (seen and unseen) in the pictures.

6. **Cloze Notes:** Provide a worksheet or slide presentation with incomplete information. During a minilecture or slide show, participants complete it with the missing data.

7. **Homework Notes:** Consider asking participants to turn their daily notes into visual notes for more extended multiday training. They can do this between sessions and then share the visual notes with partners or small groups at the next session.

8. **Swap Meet:** After participants take notes, let them share and compare with others to see how much they can add to one another's notes. This gathering of various ideas is similar to collecting random items at a swap meet or flea market.

9. **Mini-Moles:** Participants come to training with (or are provided with) a small notebook. (The name here recalls the popular Moleskin brand.) Their job is to fill in the entire notebook during training.

10. **MVP:** Participants write down the "most valuable point" from the reading, discussion, or lecture. Give the guiding prompt before the activity, which is when they'll take notes.

11. **Directed Note Taking:** Guide attendees to take relevant notes. For example, suggest they identify what agrees and doesn't agree with their experiences, make three connections to their work, or write at least one question about the topic.

12. **Toll Pass:** Participants write down what they learned in the workshop and hand in their "toll" as they finish the activity or leave training.

13. **Show Write:** Participants respond to a prompt with a short response on a piece of paper, a small whiteboard, or a gel pad. Then they all reveal their reactions simultaneously. Alternatively, each person completes the writing on a shared file projected to the training room screen.
14. **Note to a Friend:** Ask participants to think of a colleague not present today, then write a note to them summarizing the topic just covered.
15. **Pause and Apply:** After a few minutes of speaking or reading, participants pause and write down how they would apply this information in their work setting.
16. **Action Plan Starter Kit:** After every training segment, participants write one action step they'll take to implement the new learning. They should include who will do what, when it should happen, and what materials or conditions they need. By the end of the training, an entire action plan should exist.
17. **Pause and Pen:** After 10 minutes of a lecture, slide show, demonstration, discussion, or reading, participants pause and write for two minutes. Direct their writing; for example, they should summarize the points covered, list a question they have, write how to apply an idea at work, jot down an exciting issue, or copy a favorite quote.
18. **10-Word Tournament:** Participants write a 10-word sentence that summarizes the day, lecture, or section of learning. Small groups (or the whole group) then vote on their favorite sentences.
19. **Puzzle Piece:** During a break or at the end of the training, participants write down anything that's still unclear or puzzling about the training topic. Collect these notes for a quick assessment.

Although we don't entirely rule out electronic note taking, we are advocates of handwritten notes. The power of handwriting over electronic note taking is supported by research (Carter et al., 2017; Mueller & Oppenheimer, 2014; Umejima et al., 2021; Watson & Busch, 2021). During multiday workshops, we often provide this research to participants. More times than not, our thorough review of the data increases the number of people who start penning their own notes.

A written action plan provides a useful tool to promote workshop-to-worksite implementation. Some experienced trainers require participants to use a computer and draft the plans in a shared document. While people write their plans, you monitor those plans and intervene immediately if something needs to be clarified or corrected.

Speak

Just as some folks need to write in order to clarify their thinking, there are others who need to speak to form their ideas. Offer folks ample talk time to engage with one another and the training content. In addition to helping people integrate the learning, talking about the subject often helps the group build community as they get to know others' opinions and ideas.

1. **Buddy Buzz:** Pairs discuss assigned prompts: questions, summaries, connections, reflections, surprises, and so on. Biggs and colleagues (2022) recommend this strategy as one of seven primary interactive strategies for adult university instruction.
2. **Choir Response:** The entire group responds chorally to a question or prompt.
3. **Each Teach:** Partners turn and "teach" each other the essential points of what they just heard or read. Ask them to create a unique analogy or story related to the new learning.
4. **Each Test:** Partners quiz each other with questions they created from the training content.
5. **Friendly Critic:** Partners provide critical feedback on a demonstration or written product from the workshop.
6. **Point-Counterpoint:** Partners offer counterarguments to each other's points or add supporting data to their partner's line of reasoning. This structure could involve online writing in a shared document.
7. **Stadium Shout:** Participants chant, cheer, or sing a prompt the trainer provided related to the learning.

8. **Microconsulting:** In groups of three, participants follow a proto-col for troubleshooting an issue (Young & Dionne, 2020). Member A presents a problem for a few minutes while Members B and C listen and take notes. Then they ask questions for one minute. For the final two minutes, Members B and C provide suggestions while Member A listens. The roles rotate for three rounds of assistance.

9. **Table Tours:** Each team divides into "visitors" and "docents." Docents stay at the team table to explain the team's work or arti-facts. As a group, visitors rotate to other tables, take notes, and ask questions about the work they see. At each table, another team's docent explains the artifacts considered. Each visit is about 10–15 minutes. In the end, visitors return to their team table and com-pare notes with one another and the docent, identifying what strat-egies, information, and examples might benefit their team's work. We adapted this strategy from exceptional trainer Kerry Purcell (Focused Schools, 2017).

Read

Research shows that when participants read aloud to themselves or oth-ers, retention improves (Forrin & MacLeod, 2018; Noah & Colin, 2018; Watson & Busch, 2021). Some participants may not prefer reading aloud, so consider it as one option among several, and reserve it for short pas-sages or reviewing activity directions. Remember, don't hesitate to try different strategies; the more you try, the better your chances at success!

1. **Read and Code:** Announce, "Read the text and circle ____, box in ____, and underline ____." Have the code match the main points related to the topic or desired highlights from the text.

2. **Partner Read:** Partners read a passage or an article aloud; they take turns reading predetermined chunks of text. Alternatively, if one partner doesn't want to read aloud, one can read and the other can highlight key points or write a summary.

3. **Jump-In Reading:** This version of Partner Read is more sponta-neous regarding who reads when. One partner starts reading a text aloud, and the other partner jumps in and starts reading aloud at a specified point. While one reads, the other takes notes.

4. **Sticky Note Read:** Participants read and make notes on stickies. They should use various colors to indicate different concepts or trends in the reading or data. Another approach is to require a specific number of completed notes.

5. **Reason to Read:** Give participants a purpose for reading. Say, "You will read this to answer the question _____." They write their answers and share their responses with a partner as time allows. Use this strategy with video viewing or listening as well.

6. **Highlight Read:** Participants read and highlight a text's main idea or the most memorable sentence from each paragraph or passage.

7. **Read and Annotate:** Pick any note-taking format from the writing strategies, and have participants mark up the passage.

8. **Whisper Read:** Participants read aloud to themselves in a whisper.

9. **Choral or Echo Read:** Try choral or echo reading for brief texts, such as a set of directions. When used for activity directions, this strategy may decrease the need to repeat instructions.

10. **Free-Choice Read:** Participants read a passage any way they like, as long as there's visible interaction (e.g., reading aloud or reading and writing).

11. **Walk, Talk, and Read:** Allocate 10–30 minutes for participants to read aloud and talk with their fellow participants while walking around the training room. Research on the positive effects of casual walking informed this approach (Miller & Krizan, 2016). We find many people enjoy this activity as a respite from sitting all day in the training room.

Signal

An energetic way to integrate movement into the training is with the use of simultaneous signals. As with writing and talking, signals may be quick, like the flashing of an emoji sign, or longer, as with multiple-choice questions asked through a response system.

1. **High-Tech Signal:** Participants use a response system, a free texting system, electronic polling, or a projected shared document to reveal responses to a prompt.

2. **Low-Tech Signal:** Participants signal responses with color-coded cards, fingers, symbols, or gestures.
3. **Queue:** Participants stand in a row to voice their opinion: "Everyone who agrees with _____, stand on the right side of the room. Move to the left if you disagree. Those in the middle form a physical, representative continuum across the room."

Draw

Simultaneous drawing offers an alternative to writing or speaking. If you have a concept that is challenging for people to comprehend, having them draw their understanding of it might be the key to their obtaining your learning goal. Some of our favorite illustrations of concepts were derived from participants' illustrations of the idea.

1. **Draw:** Participants craft a simple visual representation of the learning. An ordinary drawing can help people recall a great deal of information (Schmeck et al., 2014; Watson & Busch, 2021). Share the most effective illustrations with the group as a way to help everyone learn the new information.
2. **Storyboard Summary:** Participants write a storyboard recap of the training using pictures and a brief narrative. Consider providing a blank storyboard template for completion.
3. **Visual Notes:** Participants write short notes using visuals. Conduct quick "show and tell" notes with partners or small groups.

Listen or Watch

During training, there is often a compelling reason for participants to watch or listen to an example or model. In these cases, keep the time sitting and just listening or watching brief: 5–10 minutes at most. Work to increase the likelihood that everyone watches or listens by providing them with something to think about or take notes on as they watch or listen.

1. **Directed Listening:** Tell participants what to listen for during the lecture, slide show, or discussion; give them something observable to do while listening. Say, "During my slide presentation, write at least three things that are new to you" or "During this discussion, let's hear finger snaps if you agree with the points made or firm knocks on the tabletop if you disagree." As mentioned in Chapter 2, this approach provides equity in a discussion since more people can provide their opinions. This maneuver is akin to using emoji reactions in online meeting platforms.

2. **Directed Viewing:** Say, "During this video, tell your partner when you see the person use the strategy we just learned" or "As you watch this model, write three things that are completed correctly, two things that need improvement, and one question you have." In short, give participants something to say or write while watching.

Expert

Require attendees to write every time they watch a video or demonstration or listen to audio. Provide a clear direction about what to watch or listen for, and verbally prompt people if you notice few are writing.

Demonstrate

Practicing live in front of peers and trainers often proves nerve-wracking for training participants. At the same time, don't let a little anxiety stop high-quality training. First, be up-front about rehearsal expectations in the goals communicated before and during workshops. Second, normalize this practice by acknowledging potential nervousness. Third, if the method you choose includes feedback, ensure participants know the feedback is intended to be a friendly critique. When you get closer to practice time, ask a volunteer to join you in front of the group so you can briefly demonstrate with a quick role play. For a comprehensive look at practice during training, check out *Practice Perfect: 42 Rules for Getting Better at Getting Better* (Lemov et al., 2012).

1. **Perform:** Participants practice the new skill or concept. Don't just show an idea and talk about it; plan for people (in pairs or trios) to rehearse it live. Having peers provide feedback is even more effective. Put the word *demonstrate* or *perform* right up front in the day's workshop goal, and remind participants about it throughout the training. This way, the performance isn't a surprise. In a workshop about assessment, for example, don't just talk about data analysis—do some data mining. In a training on coaching, don't just demonstrate a feedback conversation—practice a difficult conversation.

2. **Video Summary:** Participants produce brief video summaries with online tools (e.g., FlipGrid) or smartphone apps.

3. **Job Aide:** Participants create takeaway job aides, which provide basic, abbreviated directions for how to do something related to work. These can include memory joggers, one-pagers, tips, reminders, and so on. Participants might write reminders on a sentence strip or list the steps learned in the workshop. They should then post these notes near their desks to prompt them to apply the learning.

Expert

Send out directions for downloading and learning a simple video editing app prior to training. Then, in training, have folks make two- to three-minute video summaries. Ensure they send you a copy so you can review it and determine what learning stuck with them.

Novice

If you're not doing it already, follow the experts' lead and build participant practice into your training. It is the most effective way for you to find out if your training is working or you need to make adjustments so people understand the requirements more clearly.

Track Frequency of Engagement

Many people provide advice about how frequently trainers should engage learners. Zoom recommends interaction every five minutes during online training (Zoom, 2022). Silberman and colleagues (2015) advise active training every eight minutes. University instruction experts Biggs and colleagues (2022) find that two minutes of interaction for every 10 minutes of content results in numerous learner benefits. A highly touted study of university students recommends a minimum of every 20 minutes of learner participation (Bunce et al., 2010). We've personally witnessed many expert trainers keep participants engaged 100 percent of the training time. Even though the research findings vary, we recommend not moving forward more than about 10 minutes before *all* participants overtly engage with the content.

The frequency of participant engagement is akin to the distance between cars traveling on the highway. If we leave too much distance between us and other vehicles, another car inevitably pulls into the space. Likewise, during training, if there are large gaps of time where engagement remains unsolicited, participants find other actions to fill that time. Sometimes those activities are not productive for learning (e.g., texting, multitasking work, off-task chatting with other participants), so the savvy trainer endeavors to keep the training time and space filled with tasks that move participants toward the learning goal.

Maintain Engagement Throughout Training

One virtuoso trainer we observed, Anita Archer (Archer & Hughes, 2011), used the catchphrase "talk about, walk about, look about" as a reminder to engage and reengage learners. Trainers should explicitly *talk about* what participants need to do and how it should be done; don't infer and don't invite—just tell. But tell them nicely; avoid being mean or bullying. This approach makes expectations clear. You should also tell them why you're asking them to do what you request. Explain the research or the rationale behind each activity to increase the likelihood of cooperation (Watson & Busch, 2021).

Expert

If you're regularly getting high engagement, start targeting 100 percent engagement for 100 percent of the time. We've seen seasoned pros do this; almost every minute of the workshop people are actively writing, speaking, or demonstrating. When done well, participants often comment on the positive energy and quick pace of the training.

Novice

If full engagement during training is a daunting idea to you, then try aiming for active participation 80 percent of the workshop time from 80 percent of the people. Record yourself or ask a friend to monitor engagement for you. Most trainers who seek the 80 percent goal end up hitting 95–100 percent fairly easily.

The second aspect of Archer's advice is to *walk about* the room, which means to circulate a great deal during training. Except for directions you deliver from one regular spot, you should constantly move around the training space. Look over shoulders, listen in on conversations, check work, and clarify instructions. Tell the group early in the day that you'll be cruising throughout the training so you can provide feedback, adjust the workshop timing, and accommodate the content as necessary. A trainer's physical proximity increases group members' engagement. As mentioned in Chapter 2, doing this also allows you to select participants' responses and work products to use as exemplars.

The final component of Archer's maxim advises us to *look about* the room. Who is not focused on directions? Who is? Who is chorally responding? Who is quietly sitting? Repeat instructions or supply individual help as required to engage everyone.

Another powerhouse strategy that will help you master embedding active participation throughout training sessions is the Twin Training design adapted from Lemov (2021). With this strategy, you plan both what you will say and do and what the participants will say and do—side-by-side. Figure 3.1 provides an example of how this parallel workshop plan works.

FIGURE 3.1
Twin Training Design

Training Section	The Trainer ...	The Participants ...
Introduction	• Posts a digital sign giving directions for 3–4 activities to prepare for training: 1) Make a nametag, 2) peruse materials, 3) jot down questions about the agenda, and 4) write a personal goal for today's training. • Provides the schedule and outcomes for the day, along with norms and logistics.	• Engage in learning before training begins; this helps set the expectation that participants will interact during this workshop. • Write a personal goal aligned to the day's work. Then they share their goal with a partner.
I do	• Models a skill or provides examples and nonexamples of a concept.	• Write at least three observation notes about the model or write trends in examples and nonexamples.
We do	• Leads the practice activity using one of the structures from Chapter 1. • Provides feedback on the practice.	• Engage in the practice of writing or demonstrating with a partner. • Write and give feedback on understanding thus far to a colleague or the trainer.
You do	• Works with a struggling group, providing more explicit feedback (while most participants continue independent practice or working on the final work product in small groups).	• Practice proficiency with one another, writing and comparing work plans or working with the trainer in a small group.
Closing	• Reviews the day's goals. • Administers an evaluation.	• Revisit goals from earlier in training and write whether their personal goal was achieved or not. • Write evaluations.

Note: Add an additional column to the far right for materials and to the far left for time frames. With this, you'll have a complete trainer's plan. As needed, include more detail for oral directions, questions, and feedback. The section on Nerves in Chapter 2 suggests this Twin Training Design for the trainer anxious about presenting.

Finally, consider including a variety of engagement tactics. An assortment of participation tactics keeps the training peppy and inclusive of various learning preferences. If you continually repeat the same "write for two minutes and then turn and talk to your neighbor," you're flirting with tiresome engagement. Think of it like preparing a six-course meal where the only ingredient is Brussels sprouts.

Virtual Training Tips for Engaging Participants

- Encourage active participation. Set the expectation that participants use all features of the virtual platform to communicate (e.g., reactions, emojis, chatbox, unmute, polls, and quizzes). Provide explicit group norms about virtual participation.
- When using video, remember that all Wi-Fi and internet connections are not equal. To decrease the amount of video buffering—and subsequent lack of engagement—consider adding videos to a secure content platform and providing the link in the chatbox. This way, participants can drop out of the training platform to view videos individually and rejoin the training at a designated time. If the trainer's internet connection is unstable, try connecting the computer directly to the router instead of relying on Wi-Fi. Participants might also try a direct connection to their routers; provide advance directions for this if you anticipate a problem.
- If you plan to train online frequently, invest in a high-quality camera, light, and microphone. The enhanced quality helps keep the group's attention.
- Conduct speed sharing (Young & Dionne, 2020), a strategy in which participants are shuffled in and out of breakout rooms (with two to three people for 60–90 seconds) and they quickly partner share. Rotate through several rounds of speed sharing, assigning people new partners each round to pump energy and quick discussions into the training.
- Use online collaborative drawing tools in small groups or pairs for drawing or visual engagement (e.g., Google Drawing, Draw.io, Jamboard).
- Go low-tech in online training and ask participants to simply flash a one-word or one-phrase response on the screen.
- As with in-person training, consider using a shared document or platform for small-group or whole-group note taking. Several platforms allow for virtual building and sharing of documents (e.g., Base Camp, Dropbox, Google Docs).

- Assign texting partners for buddy buzz or partner chats. If using Zoom, assign partners to individual breakout rooms and have them individually chat with each other.
- Encourage taking notes by hand instead of on a device. Then have participants share notes with you or one another via photos or scanning apps.
- Select one of several polling programs to integrate quick quizzes in training. Plan questions at higher thinking levels. Aim for questions at DoK 2 or 3 (see Chapter 1 for more about this topic). Alter the traditional mode of multiple-choice questions by including more than one correct answer and five or more choices. This modification can keep people from guessing the correct answer and help you generate more discussions.
- To boost engagement in small groups online, keep the breakout teams small—try only three or four people per pod. Correspondingly, assign simple roles for each person, such as facilitator, note taker, timekeeper, and so on.
- If people are not discussing much, consider soliciting individual input. In small groups or through chat or text, ask them to share their comments with the whole group. Alternatively, if you know you're working with a quiet group beforehand, draft the primary training questions and send them to the group in advance; this provides more reticent people with the reflection time they might need to interact verbally with a large group.

4

Training Diplomacy

Dealing with difficult behaviors when training adults turns out to be the most frequently communicated frustration we've heard from trainers. Like a smudge refusing to abandon your glasses, challenging behaviors distort our view of ourselves and the entire workshop. Our advice for addressing these issues covers two broad areas. First, examine your training design. If troublesome behaviors continually arise during training, confirm that you're addressing adult learners' needs and that the change process receives enough attention in planning (Knowles et al., 2020; Hall & Hord, 2019). See Chapter 1 for more details. Are you providing enough practical, how-to information? Do participants connect their previous experiences with the new learning? Is it possible you're asking people to dive into deep collaboration before addressing their primary concerns about the topic? Double-check these design fundamentals to prevent many conflicts.

Second, consider the content of this chapter—a combined set of overlapping communication capacities that provide potential diplomatic responses to commonly challenging behaviors. Effective listening, facilitating discussions, fielding questions, and managing challenging behaviors all merge to create a matrix through which positive intent is the common thread (see Figure 4.1).

FIGURE 4.1
The Training Communication Matrix

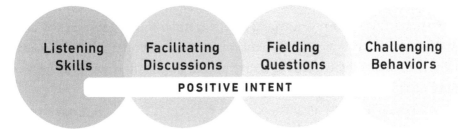

Recall that Chapter 2 provided ways to facilitate discussions and field questions. Although positive intent received some attention in the fielding questions section, we find it an overarching, invaluable principle in all situations, and it's something over which you maintain total control. Explore this chapter for details about positive intent, listening skills, and other appropriate responses to challenging conduct.

Maintain Positive Intent

A surprisingly sunny, warm spring day in San Francisco just a few years ago found us starting an all-day training for about 60 people. Plowing through the introduction and a review of group norms, we noticed a participant sitting near the front—hunched over, arms folded, with a firm scowl fixed on their face. Dana projected the vibe that they didn't want to be there; they didn't laugh or grin at any of our typically humorous remarks. We carried on. As we interacted throughout the morning, Dana refused to do group work and did almost no writing we requested, although they did complete the tiniest bit of note taking. We physically got closer to Dana's table and verbally checked in with the table group to see if they needed help or repeated directions. While everyone else acted pleased and chatty, Dana kept quiet, eyes averted, and frown fixed.

We approached Dana during the lunch break and asked how the training was going. We half-expected a barrage of how awful we were or how inappropriate the topic was to their work. Instead, Dana extolled, "This is the best training I've attended in years. I begged my supervisor to let me come when I heard about it. I got out of the hospital yesterday from surgery and can barely sit up straight, but this is wonderful. I'm sorry I can't do more of the activities; just sitting is taking all my energy. You two are wonderful; I heard you would be!" We stood there, gobsmacked and embarrassed. We confessed to Dana what we *thought* they would say and why. Everyone laughed. We were reminded that positive intent (which we didn't use with Dana) remains the presenter's best friend.

In training with a grumpy-*looking* participant, we could have considered a positive reason for the demeanor or we could have imagined a negative motivation; we did the latter. Presuming positive intent involves pretending a favorable or optimistic reason exists for a person's question, comment, or action. In *Crucial Conversations* (Patterson et al., 2021), positive intent is described as "the story behind the story" because it tells what happened and why it happened. In our case, we saw a person slumped in their chair, avoiding eye contact, scowling, and participating only minimally. Those actions provided simple facts—or "the story." Don't forget, though, there's also "the story behind the story": what we *assume* to be the reasons behind the facts—they don't want to be there, are unhappy, don't like the subject, hate us, and on and on. Keep in mind that we can make "the story behind the story" either adverse or positive. When trainers learn to assume a positive rationale for all challenges,

Novice

Positive intent takes some practice if you're not accustomed to it. For some reason, most of us tend to assume negative intent for most behaviors. To help with the shift to positive intent, try using the technique with friends, family, and colleagues—one-on-one—before attempting to articulate favorable intentions in a large, group training setting.

Novice

A great time to practice positive intent exists while you're driving. When another driver does something you object to, instead of thinking (or saying), "What an idiot," "I hate tailgaters," or "Why can't people follow the rules of the road?" try thinking, "That must be a new driver," "They're on the way to the hospital for an emergency," or "They probably didn't see that sign."

even if it's just a made-up one, they start to find themselves calming down, finding diplomacy, and courting more favorable responses from participants in return.

Positive intent is not only a concept but also a practical strategy. Figure 4.2 provides a framework for how to deploy positive intent and deal with challenging behaviors. We focus on the participant's behavior as perceived by the trainer and list it in the first column. Then we suggest the trainer take a moment and work to move from assuming a negative intent (indicated in the second column) to imagining a more positive rationale for the behavior (as noted in the third column). The trainer then decides what might be an appropriate replacement behavior for the participant in a workshop setting (the fourth column lists some examples). Finally, if the trainer feels the need to confront the issue directly, we include some sample scripts (provided in the fifth column) where the explicit use of positive intent is indicated in italics.

Expert

Take a look at your frequently asked questions or controversial topics that arise during training. Sketch out potential responses using positive intent for all the difficult questions or responses you frequently encounter. This way, when the behavior or comment arises, you're ready with a few diplomatic, positive responses.

FIGURE 4.2

Using Positive Intent as a Strategy

Participant's Action	Potential Negative Intent	Potential Positive Rationale	Appropriate Replacement Behavior	Sample Script Using Positive Intent
Yelling or being verbally aggressive with one's comments	• They're mean. • They're a bully. • They hate me. • They don't know how to control their anger.	• They are impassioned. • They have strong opinions.	• Have them speak more quietly. • Have them talk to the trainer in person instead of in front of the group.	• "You feel very strongly about this subject; so do I. Please lower your voice so we can discuss this." • "I want to hear you out. At the same time, I must ask you not to yell at me."
Engaging in side conversations during training when they should be working or listening	• They don't like the activity. • They're rude. • They were not listening when I gave directions.	• I gave bad or unclear directions. • They're an extrovert, and I'm not giving enough talk time. • There's an urgent work or personal issue that needs addressing.	• Ask if I need to be clearer. • Request they hold personal conversations during breaks. • Allow them to step out of training to manage a crisis.	• "Is there something I can clarify or help with?" • "I want to check in and ensure the training is working for you. I notice you talking to your neighbor a great deal. Do I need to put in more partner talk activities?"

Listen

Practical training necessitates strong listening skills, and most effective trainers spend their entire careers honing these skills. As much as possible, read about and practice effective listening skills. Some of the most essential factors expert trainers have told us they find critical to effective listening are listed here.

- Silence your inner voice. While listening, most of us mentally counter or refute what other people say as they speak. It's difficult to stop doing this completely, but try to quiet your inner voice (Dumbro et al., 2020). Mentally tell yourself to put your internal dialogue on pause while others are speaking.
- Keep an ear out for generalities. When someone uses words and phrases like *these kids, everyone, all the people, our partners*, and so on, it's a good idea to take a breath and ask for clarity (Costa et al., 2016). Ask, *"Who* is that?" "Do you really mean *all?"* *"Who* demanded that at your program?" Ask the question with inquisitiveness and sincerity so it doesn't come off as sarcasm. This approach helps you gently highlight a fault in someone's critical thinking by pointing out a generalization. Also, paying attention to ambiguous wording helps everyone think more precisely.
- Keep an ear out for jargon. Every occupation and industry maintains its own lexicon. Through the years, we've realized there are many misconceptions concerning terminology that most of us hear daily, such as the words *mastery* and *analysis*. One set of researchers revealed that many of our most common social disagreements derive from differing definitions of everyday vocabulary (Marti et al., 2023). There are a couple things to help mitigate the negative impact of buzzwords or lingo. When you hear a term, such as *PLC,* bantered around the training room and there appears to be confusion, stop and clarify your definition. Another approach some trainers deploy is to anticipate the terminology confusion and provide a list of key words and phrases as part of the training workbook or handouts.
- Pause. Before you start speaking, count to five silently and slowly. Occasionally, the speaker continues talking during the pause, and they often more precisely address the heart of their issue. Other benefits of wait time include higher levels of thinking, an ability to articulate concepts clearly, and a more diplomatic environment for others to join the discourse ahead (Rowe, 1986; Saphier et al., 2018).
- Acknowledge. Adults place a lot of value on experiences (Knowles et al., 2020). Therefore, simply validating someone's attitude and

personal experience goes a long way toward gaining their collaboration. We can't overstate the power of this approach enough; allow people to recognize that you seriously consider their viewpoint.

- Check your understanding. Tell the speaker you need to paraphrase or summarize what you heard. Say, "It feels like ____" or "What I understand you're saying is ____. Is that correct?" Pause after your statement and allow them to verify your understanding.
- Watch for body language. Is the individual covering their mouth, looking at the ground, or fidgeting a lot? They may want to discuss something but, for some reason, are not doing so (Hattie & Clarke, 2019; Van Edward, 2017). Directly ask, "What are your thoughts as we talk about this?" This approach may allow the person to get to the heart of an unspoken issue.

Novice

Highly proficient trainers work on effective listening for most of their career. Take that to heart. Attend trainings, read books, and find classes that teach listening skills. Make yourself a lifelong learner of listening.

Manage Challenging Behaviors

In addition to effective listening skills, positive intent, and careful training design, there are times when you may need additional strategies to properly address challenging behaviors. The following methods should help you triage—apply quick treatment to minor concerns and spend more energy dealing with significant problems. When there's a conflict with a participant, it's best to deal with the person individually, if you can, and rely on your dispositions of rapport and trust (fundamental relationship-building issues addressed in Chapter 2). Mending relationships and adjusting training design may take a lot of time. In the interim, you may need to keep the group moving forward and the training schedule on pace; the techniques in this section help you diplomatically move forward through conflict.

The following strategies should help you stay agile and address issues more quickly. Even though one (or more) of these strategies may provide enough balm to calm the relationship, you still need to follow up individually with the person and provide more listening, rapport, and care tactics. As with positive intent and listening skills, these strategies are designed to draw the challenging individual a bit closer to you and shorten the emotional distance between you. These approaches are grouped into three categories: actions to take before training, scripts or actions to take during a conflict, and follow-up tactics to use after you engaged in a challenging conversation.

> **Expert**
>
> Step out of the box of the norms you regularly see: be on time, listen to all ideas, come prepared, and so on. Set norms that the current group needs. Is there a negative climate and lots of blaming? Consider asking the group to agree to the norm "We will not disparage people or groups not in the room." Are a few folks doing all the talking? Try "We will be extremely aware of how much time we're speaking in whole group." or "We'll encourage others to share their ideas out loud." To this end, only focus on two or three targeted norms or workshop expectations at a time.

Before Training

1. **Set Norms:** Post your behavior expectations for everyone to see. Tie those expectations directly to the needs you've noted with the group. For example, "Everyone will share airtime and not use all the group speaking space for their concerns only" or "The group will focus the conversation on issues it can resolve." If you don't know the group, don't be scared to add a new norm in the middle of training (Aguilar, 2016; Mroz et al., 2018; Young et al., 2023).

2. **Meet Ahead of Time:** Before the training, seek out the person with previous challenging behaviors. Say, "In the past, you've stated

many issues with the content we'll be working on next week. I want to review the plan with you, get your input, and see if I can address any of your concerns beforehand."

3. **Address Adult Learners' Needs:** Proper planning precludes many issues with challenging behaviors. Find a way to acknowledge the person's experience with the training topic, and focus most of the training on how-to, helpful information (Knowles et al., 2020). Problems often arise when we neglect adults' unique needs, as mentioned in Chapter 1.

4. **Share the Research:** If you continually witness a common problem (e.g., multitasking, refusing to take notes by hand), produce research on the topic. Try planning a brief literature review of the research if training a group over several days and an issue is anticipated. Common topics we've observed trainers address include the impact of handwritten notes (Carter et al., 2017; Mueller & Oppenheimer, 2014; Umejima et al., 2021; Watson & Busch, 2021), the myth of multitasking (Ophir et al., 2009, Parry & Le Roux, 2021), and the myth of learning styles (Biech, 2017; Garmston, 2018; Hattie, 2023; Saphier, 2017, Saphier et al., 2018; Willingham et al., 2015). Sharing and discussing the research often assuages the problem.

During a Challenging Conversation

1. **Recognize Positive Intent:** Say, "*Many of your points are valid,* but please keep an open mind to other ideas as we move through the day" or "*I know you're excited about this idea,* but give me a chance to share my thoughts as well." In these examples, phrases in italics highlight the explicit use of positive intent. For more information, see this chapter's section on positive intent (Bailey, 2011, 2015; Costa et al., 2016; Curwin et al., 2018; Noddings, 2013; Patterson et al., 2021).

2. **Shift Prepositions:** Try to move the conversation away from complaining and toward productive action. Say, "Instead of talking *about* the district admin, let's draft a list of concerns *for*

them" or "We're not going to complain *about* ____; let's plan to speak directly *to* ____." Here, the italics highlight the shifting of prepositions.

3. **Distinguish Differences:** Respect and simply recognize basic, fundamental differences. Say, "Yours is a different and valid belief; many people hold a similar philosophy. At the same time, we're working from another theoretical basis today."

4. **Feel, Felt, Found:** Use a script to show you understand a person's perspective and see a potentially positive outcome (Gordon & Burch, 2010). Say, "You say you *feel* ____. I *felt* similarly when ____. I *found* over time I ____ [came to a different understanding, changed my thinking]." Avoid telling the person how they feel unless they explicitly state a feeling; in those instances, it's important to use the same terminology the person did. Use all three prompts for maximum impact.

5. **Value Experience:** Adults value their expertise and background (Knowles et al., 2020). Work to recognize and appreciate their prior experience while relating it to new learning. Ask, "What did you do to solve a similar problem in past situations?" Say, "This issue is like how we tackled our last new curriculum adoption. Let's look at how we managed that change so well."

6. **Talk About the Taboo:** Label the significant, bypassed issue. Say, "So, what you're saying is ____; am I right?" or "I think we're being a little too polite. I could be wrong, but I'm going to say what I think we might be thinking: ____."

7. **Ask for or Offer Help:** Solicit a person's contribution (Aguilar, 2016; Saphier et al., 2018). Ask, "What can I do now to ease your tensions?" or "For you to support this idea, what needs to happen?" Say, "Help me understand how this is such a problem" or "My experience and understanding are completely different; let's keep talking and see if we can come to some kind of agreement or solution to the issue."

8. **Facilitate Friction:** Work to get another opinion into the conversation (Aguilar, 2016). Assume disagreement is good for the

discussion. Ask, "Are you open to another idea?" or "What would be the cons of your idea?" Say, "Let's hear from someone who sees it differently" or "Talk more and see if you can convince the room this is the way to go."

9. **Use Their Name:** Even in the heat of the moment, try to use the person's name without animosity; this may establish a bit of personal connection and amity.

10. **Use Evidence:** Introduce a data point into the discussion (Young et al., 2023). Say, "When we examine your computer program usage, it does not support this point" or "Let's take a look at the work products and see what people wrote or didn't write."

11. **Forecast a Favorable Disposition:** State a disposition or attitude you're not seeing much evidence for but want to elicit. Say, "I think you're open to feedback," "I'm sure you like learning new ideas," "You'll love this next part," "I think you'll hear this easily," or "You're flexible; I've seen you adapt with your kids." It takes a bit of gumption not to come off as sarcastic, but Forecast a Favorable Disposition remains one of our favorite strategies we've seen the pros use. Often, people need to be seen differently before they'll act differently.

12. **Revisit Norms:** Review participant behavior expectations if you laid out norms beforehand (Aguilar, 2016; Mroz et al., 2018; Young et al., 2023). Stop, just momentarily, and have everyone evaluate how the group is keeping their commitment to the day's norms. Say, "For our work today, we're going to refrain from talking about team members not in the room" or "Can everyone pause a moment and evaluate how the whole team is doing with the workshop norms today?"

13. **"I don't want ____; I do want ____":** This exchange may help clarify your intent (Patterson et al., 2021). Say, "I don't want you to think I'm overcritical. I do want you to know that my remarks are meant to be helpful." "I don't want you to think I'm rushing everything. I do want you to know we only have five more minutes." "I don't want you to think I'm trying to patronize. I do want you to know I will ask you and everyone else to follow the group norms."

As with Feel, Felt, Found, you should use all the verbal stems for maximum impact.

14. **Acknowledge:** Simply restate the person's concern in as straightforward a manner as possible. Don't expand on the issue, try to explain it away, or solve the problem—just say it (Aguilar, 2016; Knowles et al., 2020; Young et al., 2023). Say, "You think this is unfair," "You don't like this new direction," or "You can't see how this would work."

15. **Pause:** Pause judiciously, and don't rush to supply a verbal response. Take a long drink of water or two. Silently count to 10. This wait time provides you and others with time to think before responding (Rowe, 1986). Say, "I'm not going to address that issue right this minute; I'll get back to you regarding what I think about what you said" or "Write your concern on the chart, and we can think about making it a topic for the next training." Not every issue needs to be addressed the moment it is raised. Don't feel bad if you don't have a retort for every difficult situation that comes up in training. Take your time, even if it's later that day or the next day, and respond when you have a clearer idea about what you really want to say.

16. **Tie Talk to Targets:** Listen carefully to what the participant says. Whenever possible, tie any aspect of their remarks to the workshop's goals; this sends the message that training goals may address their concerns. Say, "You're right, and that is part of the reason we're conducting this training today" or "This afternoon, our work will address the issues you just mentioned."

Novice

> *Overlearn* your content. Know your agenda and training material well enough that you can determine when you should address an issue immediately, when you can delay a response, and when the topic raised is inappropriate for the current training. When a challenging question or comment comes up, be in the habit of mentally passing it through the three screeners before responding.

17. **Admit Errors:** Be very, very quick to recognize when you're incorrect. Say, "I made a mistake" or "You're right. I stated it incorrectly. Thanks."

18. **Apologize:** When necessary, make sincere amends. Say, "I apologize. I didn't mean to talk over you. I'll work hard not to do that again."

    Always assume there is someone in the room who knows the content better than you do. Therefore, when this happens and you are corrected, it won't throw you off your game.

19. **Express Gratitude:** Try to find something you appreciate inside the person's remarks and be genuine with your praise (Emmons, 2016). Say, "Thanks for bringing that up; I'm sure others also wanted to know the answer," "I appreciate you speaking your mind about this," or "Thanks for bringing it to my attention."

20. **Clarify:** Listen for vague terms or venting. Know when you and the other person may have completely different understandings of the same concept (Costa et al., 2016). Ask, "Are you just venting, or do you need some solutions for the issue?" or say, "Share with me your definition of ____."

21. **Lean In:** Gently step or lean forward. Display open body language. Do not tower over the person. Do not step back or cross your arms across your chest or stomach—signs of closed body language (Van Edward, 2017).

22. **Be Curious:** Try to be curious instead of upset or silenced by challenging behavior. Work to maintain a quizzical disposition (Stone & Heen, 2014). Say, "Tell me more about this." Ask, "What led you to that conclusion?" or "What's the root cause of your position?"

23. **Try a New Example:** If you've talked a great deal about an issue, attempt to explain your point entirely differently. Provide an illustration or conduct a brief role play.

24. **Ten o'clock, Two o'clock:** Physically move so the person is in your 10:00 or 2:00 line of sight. This positioning provides you with more direct eye contact—and connection in general. This tactic comes from one of our favorite trainers: Vickie Lake.

> **Expert**
>
> You often know the sticky parts of your training: the topics where people push back or struggle. Therefore, you should be ready with two or three different ways to approach the topic. Plan for a different analogy, example, story, or illustration for the most challenging pieces of content. Use your favorite explanatory device when you first teach the concept. Then, if resistance or confusion remains, pull out one or two of your other illustrative tools to respond. You don't need half a dozen ways to explain every concept or skill you teach, but you do need a few ways to explain the most challenging topics.

25. **Talk Low and Slow:** When someone offers loud, rapid-fire comments, counter with the opposite behavior. Lower your voice and slow your speech to the pace of pouring molasses. Often, the person starts to decrease their rate and intensity to match yours.

26. **Pull Out a Chair:** Pro trainer Angela Bell Julien suggests that if a person is standing and their physical stature intimidates you, ask them to sit and face you. This seated position puts them at a much closer distance to you and symbolically reduces the disproportionate impact of their size. Suggest, "Let's have a seat; my feet are tired."

27. **Reflect and Redirect:** Reflect by acknowledging the person's concerns (Bilmes, 2012). Say, "You are unhappy with this new curriculum implementation." Then offer two positive choices: "Do you want to do this current activity by yourself or with the small group?" Sometimes, getting the person to make a simple, rational choice calms their emotional response.

28. **Applaud Approximation of Behavior:** Praise the approach to the behavior or skill you desire (Bailey, 2011, 2015). Say, with a sincere smile, "I know you're thinking about how to start the role play" or "I see you getting ready to start writing your plan." As mentioned before, that must be stated honestly and from the heart.

29. **Sway:** Slightly sway or move your hips from side to side at a rate of 60 beats per minute. Resting heart rates are 60–100 beats per

minute. Regulating your body by swaying from side to side helps you remain calm and listening, thus open to thinking through an appropriate response. As an added benefit, this behavior often helps regulate the person with the challenging behavior (Sorrels, 2015).

After a Challenging Conversation

The previous 29 strategies suggest ways to interact in the heat of the moment, right when you first encounter the behavior you don't like. Sometimes a diplomatic strategy will work to address the challenging behavior, sometimes it will not. In either case, there exist a few strategies you might attempt *after* you initially deal with the difficulty. The following tactics are designed for deployment after your initial response to the thorny encounter.

1. **Reference an Earlier Disagreement:** Let the group and person with the challenging behavior know you are unafraid of confrontation. Normalize the disagreement by waiting until later in training, when you are more relaxed, and then say something like, "This example is similar to the issue ____ and I were talking about earlier because ____." This communicates you are OK with the conflict. Additionally, it sends the message that the person is your ally in training, and the problematic conversation is helping you teach the content. If you can find humor in the connection, use it. However, do not try this if you can't convey sincere comedy, or it will come off as sarcasm.

2. **Physical Check-In:** Go to the person. Check their work, listen to their partner talk, and start a conversation. Get closer to them physically. Do not avoid them after the conflict. Your intent here is to try and establish a modicum of rapport. You're probably not going to make a new best friend, but you want the person to know you are self-assured and don't intend to avoid them. Ask them how they're doing. This physical and verbal private check-in may disarm them. We find that the most challenging people don't want one-on-one attention; this may be why they often attack from the cover of a crowd instead of waiting until a break or other times to speak to you privately.

Novice

If you're uncomfortable verbally confronting a challenging behavior from a participant, try starting with a physical check-in. Here, there's no need to address the conflict that occurred; simply walk by and check in on them or their small group. Later and with more practice, you might try resurfacing the conversation or rebooting the relationship.

3. **Resurface the Conversation:** If you can muster enough calm, dive back into the original, challenging conversation later in a more individualized setting—during a break or lunch or while others are working in small groups. Attempt something like, "I'm curious about the thinking behind what you said. Can you tell me more?" This tactic aims to jump further into the challenging conversation but in a more appropriate environment without the crowd. Frequently, the person deescalates when they are "forced" to relate with you.

4. **Reboot the Relationship:** Instead of revisiting the original, challenging conversation, work on a more relational approach. Say, "I want to check in on [or restart] our relationship because we had several disagreements earlier," "I think I'm taking a lot of airtime in our meetings, and I might have contributed to your frustration during the last whole-group discussion," or "I just wanted to check in and make sure we're OK since our last conversation." Try not to assume relationships, even challenging ones, are fixed or permanent; damage or hurt does not need to last forever. Furthermore, acknowledge that you may have contributed to the problem if, upon reflection, you think it is true.

Virtual Tips for Training Diplomacy

- Create ready responses or tip sheets for tech issues (e.g., how to mute, troubleshoot platform issues, find training materials). When encountering participants whose challenging behavior stems from using the virtual environment, send them the appropriate tip sheet via chat or email. Similarly, provide a list of FAQs, including technology issues, so the entire group can access it, and you can link to it when someone reveals frustration with training mechanics.

- Plan to have a copresenter or designated participant handling tech issues. This might involve muting a participant or establishing a quick one-on-one private meeting with them to solve technology or other problems.

- Work to get closer to participants who may need to vent or need more assistance than others. During small-group work, visit the participant in a breakout room to address any issues. Consider setting up an additional small-group room where you can meet with them individually.

- Provide an "open door" after the virtual training or during lunch breaks for participants to share their thoughts and evaluations of the training.

- Make yourself available during all breaks. Some participants may want to speak with you without the entire group listening in.

- If a vocal member continues to move conversations to issues unrelated to the training, say, "That idea might work. Let's write it down in the chat to address at the end of this meeting" or "I can discuss this more during the break."

- Create a "virtual parking lot" using a collaborative electronic document or platform for participants to post questions that will be addressed later in training, in other workshops, or during breaks.

5

Training the Trainer

The popular show *Dancing with the Stars* pairs novice dancers with professionals for a reality TV competition. The pros deploy various methods to bring their understudies up to speed—showing steps, dancing together, explaining, practicing fundamentals, repeating small dance segments endlessly, and even whispering directions during live televised performances. Many of our train-the-trainer tips mirror strategies right out of *Dancing with the Stars*.

To build the Young-Osborne Train-the-Trainer Model, we integrated our collective experience from decades of leading fruitful programs with the best advice provided by instruction researchers on scaffolded support (Archer & Hughes, 2011; Bell, 2021; Hattie, 2023; Saphier et al., 2018; Sherrington, 2019). Furthermore, we referenced several studies showing that train-the-trainer programs were efficient, were cost-effective, and improved program outcomes (Jones et al., 1977; LaVigna et al., 2005; Pearce et al., 2012; Pollnow, 2012; Suhrheinrich, 2014). We owe a debt of gratitude to our colleagues at WestEd who built train-the-trainer programs with us: Melinda Brookshire, Jan Davis, Jeanna Bilmes, and

Cynthia Dionne. Our partnerships with the California Department of Education, the California Environmental Protection Agency, and the U.S. Department of Defense Education Activity also informed this chapter.

This chapter is written for leaders or designers of train-the-trainer programs. There are two sections to the chapter. In the first, gain an overview of the six essential expectations of an effective train-the-trainer program. This section proves particularly significant if you've never conducted a train-the-trainer initiative; it will help you think through general budget and scheduling issues. In the second section, find the nitty-gritty for putting the six expectations into practice; here, more details guide the implementation of the basic program expectations. Finally, the end of the chapter sets forth tips for using technology in the context of train-the-trainer programs occurring virtually.

Prepare the Train-the-Trainer Model

Mise en place is the French phrase for prepping ingredients and equipment before cooking. It means ingredients are measured, cut, sliced, grated, and prepared in advance. Many chefs suggest that mise en place actually begins in the field where the ingredients are grown and selected. We advise similar foundational thinking with train-the-trainer programs. After a couple of decades leading several hundred people through programs, we've learned that it's possible to increase effectiveness and curtail numerous potential pitfalls with an initiative's design via thorough communication of expectations and the program description.

It's good practice to provide a contract or set of clear expectations for potential trainer candidates that outlines the scope of the work required for the program. We err on the side of providing more detail instead of less. The following list includes six train-the-trainer program expectations. As a leader, answer these six questions as you set up the initiative. Then use your responses to design the schedule and budget as well as communicate basic program expectations to potential train-the-trainer participants.

Expectation 1: What is the timeline? How many hours or days are required of trainer candidates to observe the training, conduct the training, receive feedback, and attend classes on the topic? Can time be missed or made up? What follows provides a *brief* overview of the basic train-the-trainer timeline, which is detailed more extensively in the second section of this chapter.

Event 1: Communicate "we agree" expectations to the trainer candidate. This might be completed virtually or in person. We consider this step crucial to successful train-the-trainer programs, and it is important to communicate these expectations up front to potential trainers. Why? See the detailed rationale in the next section under Conducting the Train-the-Trainer Program.

Event 2: Have the trainer candidate attend a workshop conducted by the lead trainer to learn and practice presentation skills, along with more challenging aspects of the training content. This is the "we study" step. This initial workshop event for trainer candidates provides clarity about the subject matter content and the presentation skills you expect in live training.

Event 3: Model a live training or present a recorded training session for the trainer candidate; this is the actual training that the trainer candidate eventually conducts by themselves. This step takes as long as it takes to complete the full training and is called the "I do" step. ("I" refers to the leader or expert trainer demonstrating the training.)

Event 4: Require the trainer candidate to copresent the new training with the lead trainer and receive feedback; explicit feedback is crucial (Killion & Harrison, 2004; Pearce et al., 2012). This provides the "you do, I help" part of the program ("you" refers to the trainer candidate while the lead trainer offers the help). The trainer candidate leads much of the training, and the expert (or lead trainer) assists as a copresenter. Both this and the next steps are vital to a robust train-the-trainer program and are established from the research on scaffolded support and practice with new learning (Archer & Hughes, 2011; Bell, 2021; Hattie, 2023; Lemov et al., 2012; Saphier et al., 2018; Sherrington, 2019).

Event 5: Provide time for the trainer candidate to present on their own and receive feedback from the lead trainer. This is the "you do" part of the process ("you" being the trainer candidate).

Event 6: Conduct brief, ongoing follow-up sessions with the new trainer. This we call the "you do; I advise" stage of the model. ("You" is the new trainer, and they only need general guidance from the program leader, "I.")

One of the primary reasons we structured our model around these six distinct events involved the need to progressively release responsibility from the lead trainer to the trainer candidate and enact the research on buttressing new skills (Archer & Hughes, 2011; Bell, 2021; Hattie, 2023; Saphier et al., 2018; Sherrington, 2019). For a visual representation of this process, see Figure 5.1. In this figure, as in the text, "I" refers to the expert trainer or program leader, and "you" denotes the new trainer candidate progressing through the train-the-trainer program.

FIGURE 5.1

The Young-Osborne Train-the-Trainer Model

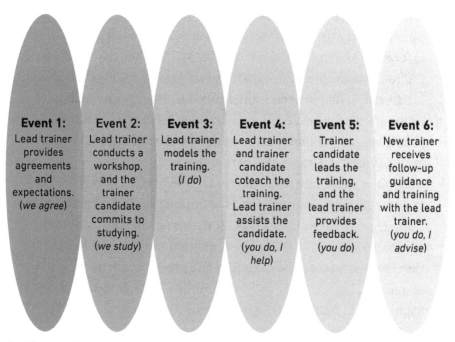

| **Event 1:** Lead trainer provides agreements and expectations. (*we agree*) | **Event 2:** Lead trainer conducts a workshop, and the trainer candidate commits to studying. (*we study*) | **Event 3:** Lead trainer models the training. (*I do*) | **Event 4:** Lead trainer and trainer candidate coteach the training. Lead trainer assists the candidate. (*you do, I help*) | **Event 5:** Trainer candidate leads the training, and the lead trainer provides feedback. (*you do*) | **Event 6:** New trainer receives follow-up guidance and training with the lead trainer. (*you do, I advise*) |

Note: The responsibility for training proficiency is increasingly transferred to the trainer candidate. "You" here refers to the individual who is learning the new training, and "I" refers to the lead trainer who is conducting the train-the-trainer program.

Expectation 2: How many individual study hours are needed? The time individual participants need to learn the training content varies, based on whether they are subject matter experts and how efficiently they commit new information to memory. It's also important to note if individual study time is compensated; if so, communicate this information to participants and budget accordingly.

Expectation 3: Are modifications to workshop activities and agendas allowed? Be clear if training materials must be memorized, reworded in the trainer's own language, or blended (i.e., some components are committed to memory, but the trainer also adds personal examples, stories, and analogies). Consider allowing candidates to include as much of their personal style and voice as possible.

Expectation 4: Will workshops on training skills or content be required? Content or subject matter experts may not always be the most compelling presenters. For this reason, we strongly urge that demonstrations and practice of training skills by the trainer candidates be baked into train-the-trainer programs. Factor in the potential need to train new trainers on *both* presentation skills and subject matter.

Expectation 5: What are the follow-up requirements? Are follow-up learning activities conducted quarterly or annually? Is there a certification component? If so, what are the requirements to maintain the certification? Draft a budget and schedule with this consideration in mind.

Expectation 6: What happens if a trainer candidate struggles or does not successfully complete the program? Most organizations maintain limited budget, time, and staffing to devote to prolonged intensive support for potential trainers. This therefore becomes an issue when a candidate fails or struggles to deliver content competently and independently. Suggestions to mitigate this issue receive detailed explanations in the next section of this chapter. Again, this issue affects staffing and budget considerations; plan accordingly.

Conduct the Train-the-Trainer Program

With the train-the-trainer program's primary expectations in place, the following section provides further details about enacting the six expectations. All combined, the following advice emanates from our experience, the work on scaffolding new learning for trainers (Archer & Hughes, 2011; Bell, 2021; Hattie, 2023; Saphier et al., 2018; Sherrington, 2019), and the research base on effective train-the-trainer programs (Jones et al., 1977; LaVigna et al., 2005; Pearce et al., 2012; Pollnow, 2012; Suhrheinrich, 2014).

Event 1: Provide Agreements and Expectations

With a completed timeline and set of program expectations, let the potential trainer candidates know those expectations up front and with as much detail as possible. Even before potential trainer candidates fully opt in to the program, the expectations help them make the decision to be involved or not. In some train-the-trainer programs, participants are simply provided with a manual with no expectation that trainers demonstrate or practice their training skills with others. Let folks know from the get-go that your program will not work that way and that there are expectations for them to study and practice. Your detailed intentions assist with "screening in" trainers eager to learn and embrace the model and "screening out" people reticent about feedback or unable to commit the time.

In the train-the-trainer process, there are three key inflection points that help you (and the trainer candidate) determine if the trainer might be successful or not:

- Acceptance of the initial program guidelines in Event 1.
- During workshop practice and demonstrations as part of Event 2.
- During the copresenting and solo presenting in Events 4 and 5.

Being explicit about critical feedback, structured support, study expectations, and time commitments in the initial program communication helps you and potential candidates decide if the initiative is a fit for them or not. Just because someone comes to you as a highly experienced and popular presenter doesn't mean they are accustomed to critical feedback on their training skills or that they are comfortable delivering training that others designed. Unambiguous program expectations communicated from the beginning help you attract candidates with the disposition and time needed for a successful program.

In the next two sections, find ideas to avoid pitfalls at two other key points in the process: demonstrations in Event 2 and presentation performance in Events 4 and 5.

Event 2: Conduct Workshop for Presentation Skills, Content, and Study Time

Begin the initiative with a day or two of workshops. Provide time to teach trainer candidates some subject matter knowledge, as needed; this may not be necessary if the trainer candidates are already subject matter experts. If they are existing subject matter experts, consider reviewing complex, challenging content to introduce potentially tricky questions they might encounter in live training. If the training content includes new information for novice trainers, make sure you build in ample study time and quizzes of the same content. Require candidates to memorize frequently asked questions from the training (if they exist) and review the training vocabulary, then conduct brief assessments on these crucial aspects of the training. Along with subject matter training, work on presentation skills: delivering training, engaging participants, managing challenging behaviors, and handling difficult questions (information found in Chapters 2–4 of this book).

Work hard to make the Event 2 workshop participatory. (See Chapter 2 for ideas on making it interactive.) Highly interactive training—group discussion, role plays, video presentations, one-on-one feedback—results in much more effective learning than passive, didactic training where candidates passively receive implementation manuals (Pearce et al., 2012).

With the aim of high participation and work on actual training performance, provide interactive activities and lots of practice. Let candidates know they will conduct demonstrations with peers and receive feedback. Chunk complex content into 10-minute scenarios that candidates can practice with one another in small groups or in front of the entire group. Then follow the mini-demonstration with feedback from peers or from expert, experienced trainers. Figure 5.2 (pp. 100–101) provides a template feedback form along with a completed example to use or adapt with trainer candidates throughout the train-the-trainer process. This is also the time to review any rubrics or performance checklists used for feedback to trainer candidates during the entire program.

In addition to providing learning support, the mini-demonstrations help you and the trainer candidates decide who needs additional support moving forward. This activity of producing training, even in front of supportive colleagues, may produce anxiety for some candidates. Even so, they should be able to produce small amounts of high-quality training. If they cannot, this should be a red flag for you; it is time to start providing extra support immediately. This is one of the inflection points mentioned earlier. Give them more one-on-one time with you. Give explicit feedback on what needs to be corrected and when. Offer extra study time, if possible. In some cases, the trainer candidate may request extra support following an unsuccessful mini-demonstration even before you suggest it; be prepared to help them with concrete strategies.

This initial workshop is also the "we study" part of the train-the-trainer model, where both guided group study and independent study time are provided. Our experience revealed that inadequate study time was the primary reason some participants failed to complete train-the-trainer programs. New trainers frequently underestimate the amount of time required to learn the training, *especially if the subject matter content is new to them.* Avoid this pitfall by detailing, in the initial expectations, the amount of study time required and by providing on-the-clock study time. A couple of agencies we worked with offered candidates two days of paid study time because the training content was new for everyone. In these cases, the lead trainers asked everyone to study at home or in the office. Then, once a day, on both days, the entire group gathered online to debrief what they studied, answer common questions, and share study tips. The training leaders remained online the entire time and provided virtual office hours during which individuals or small groups of trainer candidates could sign up for one-on-one consults.

If you are providing the candidates with a canned training—training that is already produced and must be delivered without changes—then be ready for people to struggle with it. As one trainer candidate remarked, "Training with another person's workshop materials is a bit like wearing someone else's shadow." This type of training may require more study time. If possible, allow some modifications to a predesigned workshop; this provides trainers with a bit of control and choice involving the new learning. Allowing adults some latitude in training delivery addresses one of the basic needs of adult learners—the desire for a bit of control or choice—as mentioned in Chapter 1 (Biech, 2017; Knowles et al., 2020; NASEM, 2018).

Every training is different and budget constraints drive some of the decisions, but we typically take one or two days to conduct the "we study" workshop. During this time, in addition to training on basic presentation skills, we require one round of a 10-minute presentation on some challenging aspect of the training and provide individual feedback on this mini-demonstration. Then we require a second round of presenting that same exact content, but this second time, trainer candidates must include the changes we recommended in the feedback session. The primary objective with this second round of demonstrations is to ascertain who implements the feedback and who does not. The latter group is folks who need extra support for the remainder of the process.

Event 3: Model the Training for Trainer Candidates

Soon after the initial workshop, ideally the next day, trainer candidates watch a model training session (live or recorded). In terms of train-the-trainer design, this is considered the "I do" step; the leader provides a model of the ideal training. Candidates analyze the training subject matter and the presentation skills as they observe. Place the candidates to the side or in the back of a live session. While one seasoned trainer leads the live training, another leader periodically gathers candidates outside the training room to analyze their observations of the live training. If live training cannot be arranged or you don't have two expert trainers, try substituting a video model and following the same process for this event.

It's important to sequence Event 3 *after* Event 2. During the Event 2 workshop, the trainer candidates are instructed to pay attention to specific details during the Event 3 model of training. In the Event 2 workshop, you establish specific training and content expectations.

FIGURE 5.2

Example Trainer Feedback Form

Date:	Presentation Topic:

Name:

Observation Notes

Effective Practices:

Issues to Correct:

Note if the following were present and to what degree. How could the element be improved?

Content Is Correct	Directions Are Explicit	Interactive Reading Strategies	Fielding Questions

Date:	Presentation Topic: Background Research

Name: Danuzia

Observation Notes

Effective Practices:
- Begins with gaining attention (uses call & respond: Trainer: You ready? Participants: I'm ready).
- Models document needed for activity by holding it up, "You will need the purple handout from your folder." Scans the group to ensure all have it up.
- Uses break-in read to share the "five stages of language development."
- Identifies all stages correctly. Asks participants to share an example of each stage.
- Responds to questions about the content and clarifies expectations.
- Corrects incorrect information.

Issues to Correct:
- Stop roaming around the room while providing directions. And directions need to be explicit and sequential. "First, take out the purple handout and then find the article on language development. We don't need it now. Next, work with a partner, and complete the chart on the back using the information you need to read on pages 3–4."
- Didn't let participants know the activity was coming to an end. The activity ended without warning. Providing notice is helpful because it allows participants time to finish their writing or thoughts and prepare themselves for the next piece of content.
- When responding to participants' questions, be careful to avoid verbal fillers like "um." When discussing the assessment, you said "um" 12 times. Memorize the FAQs so you can respond to those questions more confidently and see the other workshop tips for avoiding pause fillers.

Note if the following were present and to what degree. How could the element be improved?

Content Is Correct	Directions Are Explicit	Interactive Reading Strategies	Fielding Questions
Yes, continue to provide correct content!	Stay in one spot and include timeframes. Work on the sequence of steps in directions. For example, "First, read the article; now take out the handout. Next, work with a partner to complete the activity." Near the end of the activity, say, "There are three more minutes!"	Used one strategy (choral read). Include another interactive reading tactic for the article. Try "pause and write," "partner read," or "walk and read."	All information provided to participants was correct and questions were thoroughly addressed. Keep this up! Do work to reduce the use of "um" when fielding questions.

With this knowledge in hand, the trainer candidates are directed to observe the lead trainer and pay attention to the subtle tactics they use to present or to convey the content—practices they might have missed before being told.

Event 4: Copresent the Training with the Trainer Candidate

This train-the-trainer stage provides the "you do, I help" event. Trainer candidates coteach or copresent with a lead trainer. At this point, it's good practice to ask trainer candidates to take on the more difficult parts so there's a gradual shift of responsibility in ownership of the training content. Regarding copresenting formats, consider structures adapted from DeRuvo (2010) that the lead trainer and trainer candidate might use:

- **Rotate turns** so one person leads the presentation while the other roams and monitors participants, clarifying directions and assisting people as needed. Switch roles throughout the day. This is the most typical model of copresenting we observe. This may help the trainer candidate ease into the training because they are not responsible for every single training activity.
- **Sidebar present** is where one person leads instruction while the other models note taking or completing a graphic organizer for the group. The sidebar presenter might ask "naive" questions (questions the participants should be asking but are not) or make explanatory comments from the side of the room. This structure of presenting proves effective as it allows the trainer candidate to lead most of the content of the training while leaving space for the expert trainer to jump in and help as needed.
- **Parallel present** occurs when each presenter simultaneously works with a different small group of adults during the same training time and in the same space. It might help a struggling trainer manage a smaller group instead of the whole group in the beginning stages of learning new training.
- **Team present** takes place when both presenters lead the learning simultaneously. They lead and interject like a jazz duet without an apparent leadership shift. That said, the trainer candidate should assume more of the lead in the training.

No matter which copresenting format is used, the lead trainer can always jump in if the candidate gets stuck or encounters a challenging question they can't manage. Feedback and coaching from the lead trainer occur away from and out of earshot of participants. To help with this feedback, apply observation checklists or rubrics to assess candidates' performance. We've found it extremely valuable to be very specific about what we're looking for. Provide examples and nonexamples of desired outcomes for content delivery. Figure 5.3 offers a partial rubric for one training component: content delivery. Notice how you might adapt this type of performance indicator to include other criteria.

Work to provide explicit feedback throughout the train-the-trainer process. During the "we study" workshop, provide feedback to both the group and individuals following their practice demonstrations. During the "you do, I help" and "you do" events, provide constructive criticism both briefly during training and more thoroughly after training. We developed a straightforward, research-based process for providing critical notes that

FIGURE 5.3

Partial Rubric for Presentation Skills

Training Content		
Needs Coaching and Repeating Training Presentation	**Acceptable**	**Strong**
• The candidate delivers misinformation. • The candidate reads directly from notes or slides most of the time. • The candidate mixes up training terminology. • The lead trainer must intervene to correct misinformation.	• Information is accurate. • Candidate's stories and analogies are logical to the content. • The candidate reads from notes only occasionally. • The candidate can connect participants' comments correctly to the training content.	• All the information is correct. • Candidate's stories and analogies make the content more comprehensible. • The candidate makes appropriate connections between the different segments of the training. • The candidate provides a rationale for each activity.

Note: This example is only part of one rubric for content. We use additional rubrics for the quality of directions, handling participant questions, and other topics.

is based on our work with coaching conversations (Hattie & Clarke, 2019; Stone & Heen, 2014; Young et al., 2023). First, provide positive descriptive appreciation for the effective practices observed. In this stage, explicitly state what was positive and why it was effective. With the more critical notes, state the ineffective practice and then brainstorm solutions to improve, such as "Participants sat for 30 minutes without being engaged in the content. Using tactics learned in the 'we study' workshop, what could you have done differently to get people interacting with the information?" Have the candidate set a plan of action and look for improvement at the next available opportunity. Try not to overwhelm new trainer candidates; focus only on three or four major critiques during each round of feedback while providing abundant appreciation for effective performance skills.

Even with precise feedback and the support of copresenting, some new trainers may still struggle. Remember both Event 4, copresenting, and Event 5, solo presenting, are key places to determine if the candidate might successfully complete the process. Be prepared with additional support if needed and possible (e.g., more rounds of copresenting, more time to study).

Event 5: Allow the Trainer Candidate to Present on Their Own

When the trainer candidate presents on their own during this "you do" day, the lead trainer should stay off stage and observe. The candidate conveys all content, delivers high-quality training skills, and manages all questions and behaviors throughout the session. The lead trainer may conduct minimal whisper-coaching during training or at breaks, but more robust feedback happens after the training session.

At this point in the process, we find the candidate either internalized the content and performed at a high level or was so nervous that another course of action may be necessary before moving forward. Before the "you do" day, decide what course of action you'll take if a presenter does not perform to satisfaction. Will there be another opportunity to repeat the day? Sometimes, that is all the person needs to be successful: two or three repetitions. Don't be alarmed if this is the case for a few trainer candidates. Will additional coaching support be implemented (and have you budgeted for this expense)? It is essential to be as transparent as possible with trainer-candidates about expectations before this day. Out of a group of 20 potential trainer candidates, it is likely that one or two require more support than the remainder of the group.

This is one of the most challenging issues we've experienced, and we've heard similar comments from other leaders of train-the-trainer programs: "I have a candidate who cannot meet our basic requirements as a trainer." Before launching the program, decide how many attempts candidates are allowed to achieve basic proficiency and at what stage in the process they are required to demonstrate the training independently and with fidelity. As a program leader, draft a clear plan for exiting trainer candidates from the program if they cannot meet the minimum requirements. In the plan, establish minimum requirements for trainer candidates to display proficiency. We highly recommend rubrics for this purpose. Also, identify who communicates the adequate or inadequate completion to the trainer candidate and at what point in the program this decision occurs. Communicate these expectations from the beginning.

Event 6: Provide Follow-Up Guidance and Training

The train-the-trainer program's final phase should involve a gesture of closure and some form of follow-up. Once the process is complete, the newly minted trainer can be presented with a certificate of completion or another form of special recognition. We recommend acknowledging the trainer's hard work and diligence in a befitting manner.

The act of maintaining the role of trainer should be extended with further follow-up requirements. Consider how the new trainer continues to demonstrate their knowledge. Is there a requirement to deliver a minimum number of training sessions per year? Will they occasionally copresent with the lead trainer? Are they expected to submit feedback from the practitioners they trained? As a new trainer, they are responsible for staying abreast of changes to the material and updates to regulations. How will they do that? See ideas in Chapter 1 for potential follow-up activities. Some activities other program leaders incorporated included group book studies on listening skills, video reviews of challenging training components, and training idea exchanges among the trainers. These sessions transpire in-person or virtually, annually or semiannually, and last between one and six hours.

"I trained for decades, and I teach community college. This is the first time in my career I received critical, precise feedback about my training skills. This was invaluable." This comment from an experienced trainer in St. Louis echoes similar responses regarding our train-the-trainer model. In our work, this final phase of the model may offer a new chapter in people's professional development and training lives. The new trainer is now prepared to provide engaging, research-based professional development for adults in a manner that promotes the importance of adult learning theory through effective learning strategies. Our train-the-trainer model is not only rigorous in the study of specific content but also meticulous in terms of weaving adult learning theory, the change process, engagement, instructional prowess, and effective instructional design into a tapestry of training.

Virtual Tips for Train-the-Trainer Programs

- Plan to incorporate a "Technology 101" session to review the functions of the online platform, either before a virtual event or as a part of the "we study" workshop. Prepare the group for all the online features; you don't want the workshop to become a technology how-to course.
- Provide materials in both electronic and paper format. Provide participants with paper documents beforehand. Encourage them to decide how they want to interact with the materials, electronically or on paper, in advance.
- Host a 30-minute synchronous virtual session before the actual event. This virtual prelaunch allows participants to meet one another and discuss the process. It can also include introductions and goals for the train-the-trainer event. Questions and relationships organically formed during in-person training may not happen in virtual events unless the environment is created intentionally.

Create such a community with a prelaunch meeting and more community builders sprinkled throughout the program.

- To keep interaction high and allow time for ample feedback, keep the virtual groups smaller than 10 participants. In virtual events, participants tend to require more time to gather their thoughts and engage in conversations; plan accordingly.
- Provide open-door sessions for trainer candidates on a monthly or bimonthly basis as they move through the train-the-trainer program. These informal sessions allow candidates to stay connected and discuss where they are in the process. In some cases, the train-the-trainer process may take more than six months to complete. If participants have a designated time and space to connect, it increases the likelihood of success. If these sessions are included, be sure to earmark necessary funds and personnel .
- Create "traditions" for the team to expect. For instance, start each session with a song or end each session with a particular poem, quote, or joke for the day. This promotes much-needed camaraderie in an online world. Alternatively, make participants responsible for beginning or ending the sessions to increase the virtual group community.

Concluding Thoughts

If you slid among alternate realities like protagonist Evelyn Wang in the movie *Everything Everywhere All at Once,* how would you view yourself as a trainer? Are you occasionally extraordinary? Do you sometimes flail about a bit? Would you merit applause at the end of a workshop and then later realize no one picked up what you were throwing down? Are you a combination of all those successes and failures at once? Regardless of the perspective on your performance as a trainer, we hope that if you stuck with this small book, you've reflected on your repertoire of training skills and added some best practices and deleted some tired, ineffective traditions. Now, what are your next steps?

Our desire is that you'll prove an adventurous trainer practitioner and start experimenting with training skills ASAP. You have the tools and ideas now! If you don't want to revamp your training wholesale, then start with a few tactics from Chapter 2 to make your current training more participatory. Get folks talking and moving. Look at the training design and see if you can sneak in at least a tiny practice session or a make-and-take approach with your next workshop. Plan to deploy a new script the next time you encounter an undesired participant behavior.

Do you want to make a major impact on your training? Then take a hard look at the training agenda and shift from a random arrangement of activities to a powerful session where folks walk away with new skills or a new understanding because of a coherent, engaging workshop event. Or test out a new strategy for follow-up and see if you can secure a little higher implementation after training. Start with a clear picture of what training follow-up will look like, and thoughtfully plan your workshop backward from there.

For such a gregarious endeavor, sometimes leading training feels lonely, especially in instances where few people comprehend your targets, or a carefully thought-out activity just flops, or minimal learning sticks after training. That isolation compounds when you know no one else (who does exactly what you do) who you can bounce ideas off. In those times, use this book as a silent guide—a speechless coach, if you will. If you feel like you've grown hot dogs for fingers (yes, that's another nod to *Everything Everywhere All at Once*) and your workshop outcomes are making no sense to you, think back to "that little presentation skills book" you just read and unearth some ideas to empower training participants to learn, engage, and implement. With fingers crossed (even hot dog fingers) and a bit of hard work, you'll be back on track to highly effective and exciting workshops in no time.

Happy training!

References

Aguilar, E. (2013). *The art of coaching: Effective strategies for school transformation.* Jossey-Bass.

Aguilar, E. (2016). *The art of coaching teams: Building resilient communities that transform schools.* Jossey-Bass.

Allen, D., & Eve, A. (1968). Microteaching. *Theory into Practice, 7*(5), 181–185.

Allen, J. A., & Rogelberg, S. G. (2013). Manager-led group meetings: A context for promoting employee engagement. *Group & Organization Management, 38,* 543–569.

Anderson, L. W., & Krathwohl, D. R. (2001). *A taxonomy for learning, teaching, and assessing: A revision of Bloom's taxonomy of educational objectives.* Longman.

Archer, A. L., & Hughes, C. A. (2011). *Explicit instruction: Effective and efficient teaching.* Guilford.

Bailey, B. (2011). *Managing emotional mayhem: The five steps for self-regulation.* Loving Guidance.

Bailey, B. (2015). *Conscious discipline: Building resilient classrooms.* Loving Guidance.

Bell, M. (2021). *The fundamentals of teaching: A five-step model to put the research evidence into practice.* Routledge.

Biech, E. (2017). *The art and science of training.* ADT.

Biggs, J., Tang, C., & Kennedy, G. (2022). *Teaching for quality learning at university: What the student does* (5th ed.). Open University Press.

Bilmes, J. (2012). *Beyond behavior management: The six life skills children need to thrive in today's world* (2nd ed.). Redleaf.

Bloom, G., Castagna, C., Moir, E., & Warren, B. (Eds.). (2005). *Blended coaching: Skills and strategies to support principal development.* Corwin.

Bunce, D. M., Flens, E. A., & Neiles, K. Y. (2010). How long can students pay attention in class? A study of student attention decline using clickers. *Journal of Chemical Education, 87*(12), 1438–1443.

Cain, S. (2013). *Quiet: The power of introverts in a world that can't stop talking.* Random House.

California Department of Education. (2023). Desired results training and technical assistance project from the California Department of Education, child development division, with WestEd Center for Child and Family Studies. [workshop materials].

Carpenter, S. K., & Toftness, A. R. (2017). The effect of prequestions on learning from video presentations. *Journal of Applied Research in Memory and Cognition, 6*(1), 104–109.

Carter, S. P., Greenberg, K., & Walker, M. S. (2017). The impact of computer usage on academic performance: Evidence from a randomized trial at the United States Military Academy. *Economics of Education Review, 56,* 118–132.

Chhokar, J. S., Brodbeck, F. C., & House, R. J. (Eds.). (2019). *Culture and leadership across the world: The GLOBE book of in-depth studies of 25 societies* (2nd ed.). Psychology Press.

Costa, A. L., Garmston, R. J., Hayes, C., & Ellison, J. (2016). *Cognitive coaching: Developing self-directed leaders and learners* (3rd ed). Rowman & Littlefield.

Cowan, N. (2000). The magical number 4 in short-term memory: A reconsideration of mental storage capacity. *Behavioral and Brain Sciences, 24*(1), 87–185.

Curwin, R. L., Mendler, A. N., & Mendler, B. D. (2018). *Discipline with dignity: How to build responsibility, relationships, and respect in your classroom* (4th ed). ASCD.

Damisch, L., Stoberock, B., & Mussweiler, T. (2010). Keep your fingers crossed! How superstition improves performance. *Psychological Science, 21*(7), 1014–1020.

Darling-Hammond, L., Flook, L., Cook-Harvey, C., Barron, B., & Osher, D. (2020). Implications for the educational practice of the science of learning and development. *Applied Developmental Science, 24*(2), 97–140.

DeRuvo, S. (2010). *The essential guide to RTI: An integrated, evidence-based approach.* Jossey-Bass.

Dumbro, A. L., Jablon, J., & Stetson, C. (2020). *Coaching with powerful interactions: How to connect with children to extend their learning* (2nd ed.). National Association for the Education of Young Children.

Easton, L. B. (Ed.). (2015). *Powerful designs for professional learning.* Learning Forward.

Ebbinghouse, H. (1964). *Memory: A contribution to experimental psychology.* Dover. (Originally published 1885).

Emmons, R. (2016). *The little book of gratitude: Create a life of happiness and wellbeing by giving thanks.* Gia.

Fiorella, L., & Mayer, R. E. (2016). Effects of observing the instructor draw diagrams on learning from multimedia lessons. *Journal of Educational Psychology, 108,* 528–546.

Fishbach, A., & Finkelstein, S. R. (2020). Feedback and goal pursuit: How feedback influences persistence, disengagement, and change in goal pursuit. In H. Aarts & A. Elliot (Eds.), *Goal-directed behavior: The concept of action in psychology* (pp. 203–230). Routledge.

Focused Schools. (2017, May). Instructional leadership team professional development for staff at Alliance College-Ready Schools in Los Angeles, CA. [workshop materials].

Fong, C. J., Patall, E. A., Vasquez, A. C., & Stautberg, S. (2018). A meta-analysis of negative feedback on intrinsic motivation. *Educational Psychology Review, 31*(1), 121–162.

Forrin, N. D., & MacLeod, C. M. (2018). This time it's personal: The memory benefit of hearing oneself. *Memory, 26*(4), 574–579.

Garmston, R. J. (2018). *The presenter's fieldbook: A practical guide* (3rd ed.). Rowman & Littlefield.

Gordon, T., & Burch, N. (2010). *Teacher effectiveness training: The program proven to help teachers bring out the best in students of all ages.* Three Rivers.

Hale, J., & Grenny, J. (2020, March 9). How to get people to actively participate in virtual meetings. [blog post]. https://hbr.org/2020/03/how-to-get-people-to-actually-participate-in-virtual-meetings

Hall, G., & Hord, S. (2019). *Implementing change: Patterns, principles, and potholes* (5th ed.). Pearson.

Hammond, Z. (2015). *Culturally responsive teaching and the brain: Promoting authentic engagement and rigor among culturally and linguistically diverse students.* Corwin.

Haring, N. G., Lovitt, T. C., Eaton, M. D., & Hansen, C. L. (1978). *The fourth R: Research in the classroom.* Merrill.

Hattie, J. (2018). Hattie ranking: 252 influences and effect sizes related to student achievement. *Visible Learning.* https://visible-learning.org

Hattie, J. (2023). *Visible learning, the sequel: A synthesis of over 2,100 meta-analyses relating to achievement.* Routledge.

Hattie, J., & Clarke, S. (2019). *Visible learning: Feedback.* Routledge.

Himmele, P., & Himmele, W. (2017). *Total participation techniques: Making every student an active learner.* (2nd ed.). ASCD.

House, R. J., Dorfman, P. W., Javidan, M., Hanges, P. J., & Sully de Luque, M. F. (2014). *Strategic leadership across cultures: GLOBE study of CEO leadership behavior and effectiveness in 24 countries.* SAGE.

Institute on Trauma and Trauma-Informed Care (ITTIC). (2015). What is trauma-informed care? School of Social Work, University at Buffalo. http://socialwork.buffalo.edu/social-research/institutes-centers/institute-on-trauma-and-trauma-informed-care/what-is-trauma-informed-care.html

Jones, F. H., Fremouw, W., & Carples, S. (1977). Pyramid training of elementary school teachers to use a classroom management "skill package." *Journal of Applied Behavior Analysis, 10,* 239–253.

Joyce, B., & Showers, B. (2002). *Student achievement through staff development.* ASCD.

Katzir, M., Emanuel, A., & Liberman, N. (2020). Cognitive performance is enhanced if one knows when the task will end. *Cognition, 197,* 104–189.

Kauffeld, S., & Lehmann-Willenbrock, N. (2012). Meetings matter: Effects of team meetings on team and organizational success. *Small Group Research, 43,* 130–158.

Killion, J. (2019). *The feedback process: Transforming feedback for professional learning* (2nd ed.). Learning Forward.

Killion, J., & Harrison, C. (2004). Training the trainer. In L. B. Easton (Ed.), *Powerful designs for professional learning* (pp. 231–236). National Staff Development Council.

Knowles, M. S., Holton, E. F., Swanson, R. A., & Robinson, P. A. (2020). *The adult learner: The definitive classic in adult education and human resource development* (9th ed.). Routledge.

Koch, G. E., Paulus, J. P., & Coutanche, M. N. (2020). Neural patterns are more similar across individuals during successful memory encoding than during failed memory encoding. *Cerebral Cortex, 30*(7), 3872–3883.

Kounin, J. S., & Sherman, L. W. (1979). School environments as behavior settings. *Theory into Practice, (18)*3, 145–151.

Ladson-Billings, G. (2021). *Culturally relevant pedagogy: Asking a different question (culturally sustaining pedagogies series).* Teachers College Press.

LaVigna, G. W., Christian, L., & Willis, T. J. (2005). Developing behavioral services to meet defined standards with a national system of specialist education services. *Pediatric Rehabilitation, 8,* 144–155.

Lemov, D. (2021). *Teach like a champion 3.0: 63 techniques that put students on the path to college.* Jossey-Bass.

Lemov, D., Woolway, E., & Yezzi, K. (2012). *Practice perfect: 42 rules for getting better at getting better.* Jossey-Bass.

Leong, K., Sung, A., Au, D., & Blanchard, C. (2021). A review of the trend of microlearning. *Journal of Work-Applied Management, 13*(1), 88–102.

Little, J. W. (1993). Professional community in comprehensive high schools: The two worlds of academic and vocational teachers. In J. Little & M. McLaughlin (Eds.), *Teacher's work: Individuals, colleagues, and contexts* (pp. 137–163). Teachers College Press.

Maki, K. E., Moody, M. E., Cullins, S. L., & Griffin, T. L. (2022 July 28). Examination of a modified incremental rehearsal approach to explore causal mechanisms. *Journal of Behavioral Education,* 1–24.

Malamed, C. (2015). *Visual design solutions: Principles and creative inspiration for learning professionals.* Wiley.

Marti, L., Wu, S., Piantadosi, S. T., & Kidd, C. (2023). Latent diversity in human concepts. *Open Mind: Discoveries in Cognitive Science, 7,* 79–92.

Miller, J. C., & Krizan, Z. (2016). Walking facilitates positive affect (even when expecting the opposite). *Emotion, 16*(5), 775–785.

Moreno, R., & Mayer, R. E. (2000). A coherence effect in multimedia learning: The case for minimizing irrelevant sounds in the design of multimedia instructional messages. *Journal of Educational Psychology, 92*(1), 117–125.

Mroz, J. E., Allen, J. A., Verhoeven, D. C., & Shuffler, M. L. (2018). Do we really need another meeting? The science of workplace meetings. *Current Directions in Psychological Science, 27*(6), 484–491.

Mueller, P. A., & Oppenheimer, D. M. (2014). The pen is mightier than the keyboard: Advantages of longhand over laptop note taking. *Psychological Science, 23,* 1159–1168.

National Academies of Sciences, Engineering, and Medicine (NASEM). (2018). *How people learn II: Learners, contexts, and cultures.* National Academies Press.

Noah, D. F., & Colin M. M. (2018). This time it's personal: The memory benefit of hearing oneself. *Memory, 26*(4), 574–579.

Noddings, N. (2013). *Caring: A relational approach to ethics and moral education* (2nd ed.). University of California Press.

Odermatt, I., König, C. J., Kleinmann, M., Bachmann, M., Röder, H., & Schmitz, P. (2018). Incivility in meetings: Predictors and outcomes. *Journal of Business and Psychology, 33,* 263–282.

Ophir, E., Nass, C., & Wagner, A. D. (2009). Cognitive control in media multitaskers. *Proceedings of the National Academy of Sciences, 106*(37), 15583–15587.

Parry, D. A., & Le Roux, D. B. (2021). "Cognitive control in media multitaskers" ten years on: A meta-analysis. *Cyberpsychology: Journal of Psychosocial Research on Cyberspace, 15*(2), 1–26.

Patterson, K., Grenny, J., Switzler, A., & McMillan, R. (2021). *Crucial conversations: Tools for talking when stakes are high* (3rd ed.). McGraw-Hill.

Pearce, J., Mann, M. K., Jones, C., van Buschbach, S., Olff, M., & Bisson, J. I. (2012). The most effective way of delivering a train-the-trainers program: A systematic review. *Journal of Continuing Education in the Health Professions, 32*(3), 215–226.

Pollnow, M. (2012). *Implementing a K-12 train the trainer professional development model through the school improvement grant.* (Publication No. 3505956) [doctoral dissertation, Arizona State University]. ProQuest Dissertations Publishing.

Rowe, M. B. (1986). Wait time: Slowing down may be a way of speeding up? *Journal of Teacher Education, 37,* 43–50.

Saphier, J. (2017). *High expectations teaching: How we persuade students to believe and act on "smart is something you can get."* Corwin.

Saphier, J., Haley Speca, M., & Gower, R. R. (2018). *The skillful teacher: The comprehensive resource for improving teaching and learning* (7th ed.). Research for Better Teaching.

Schmeck, A., Mayer, R. E., Opfermann, M., Pfeiffer, V., & Leutner, D. (2014). Drawing pictures during learning from scientific text: Testing the generative drawing effect and the prognostic drawing effect. *Contemporary Educational Psychology, 39*(4), 275–286.

Sherrington, T. (2019). *Rosenshein's principles in action.* John Catt Educational Limited.

Silberman, M., Biech, E., & Auerbach, C. (2015). *Active training: A handbook of techniques, designs, case examples, and tips* (4th ed.). Wiley.

Smutny, M. (2019). *THRIVE: The facilitator's guide to radically inclusive meetings.* Civic Reinventions.

Social Programs That Work (SPTW). (2021). Evidence summary for the Perry Preschool Project. https://evidencebasedprograms.org/programs/perry-preschool-project

Sorrels, B. (2015). *Reaching and teaching children exposed to trauma.* Gryphon House.

Stone, D., & Heen, S. (2014). *Thanks for the feedback: The science and art of receiving feedback well.* Viking.

Suhrheinrich, J. (2014). A sustainable model for training teachers to use pivotal response training. *Autism, 19*(6), 713–723.

Umejima, K., Ibaraki, T., Yamazaki, T., & Sakai, K. L. (2021). Paper notebooks vs. mobile devices: Brain activation differences during memory retrieval. *Frontiers in Behavioral Neuroscience, 15,* 1–11.

Van Edward, V. (2017). *Captivate: The science of succeeding with people.* Penguin Random House.

Wammes, J. D., Ralph, B. C. W., Mills, C., Bosch, N., Duncan, T. L., & Smilek, D. (2019). Disengagement during lectures: Media multitasking and mind wandering in university classrooms. *Computers & Education, 132,* 76–89.

Watson, E., & Busch, B. (2021). *The science of learning: 99 studies that every teacher needs to know.* Routledge.

Webb, N. L. (2002). *Alignment study in language arts, mathematics, science, and social studies of state standards and assessments for four states.* Council of Chief State School Officers.

Webb, N. L. (2012, December). *Content complexity for mathematics and science instructional planning.* Presentation at Florida Center for Research in Science, Technology, Engineering, and Mathematics at Florida State University. http://facstaff.wcer.wisc.edu/normw/AERA%20Page1.htm

Wegner, D. M., Schneider, D. J., Carter, S. R., & White, T. L. (1987). Paradoxical effects of thought suppression. *Journal of Personality and Social Psychology, 53*(1), 5–13.

WestEd. (2016, January). Coach for success and teach for success training presented to Goodland Elementary School staff in Racine, WI. [workshop materials].

Willingham, D. T., Hughes, E. M., & Dobolyi, D. G. (2015). The scientific status of learning styles theories. *Teaching of Psychology, 42*(3), 266–271.

Young, A. K., & Dionne, C. (2020). *Engage virtually: 100+ tactics for presenting & meeting.* Training presented online for Valley View School District 365. [workshop materials].

Young, A. K., Julien, A. B., & Osborne, T. (2023). *The instructional coaching handbook: 200+ troubleshooting strategies for success.* ASCD.

Zenger, J., & Folkman, J. (2014). Your employees want the negative feedback you hate to give. *Harvard Business Review Blog Network.* [blog post] https://hbr.org/2014/01/your-employees-want-the-negative-feedback-you-hate-to-give

Zoom. (2022). Zoom online event best practices guide. https://support.zoom.us/hc/en-us/articles/209743263-Zoom-Webinars-and-Zoom-Meetings-best-practices

Index

The letter *f* following a page locator denotes a figure.

About the Authors

A. Keith Young is a writer and a trainer of school administrators, teacher coaches, and instructional leadership teams. Originally from Hokes Bluff, Alabama, Keith was a first-generation college graduate and taught secondary students English and math for the U.S. government overseas. In his first years of teaching, he developed a knack for training colleagues in school improvement. Training and coaching from prominent educational leaders—Jon Saphier, Louise Thomson, Ernie Stokowski, Robby Champion, Rick DuFour, and Robert Garmston, among others— provided him with a solid and diverse background in instruction and coaching. After working as a school turnaround principal, he worked for the California nonprofit education and research agency WestEd. Keith maintains a teaching style that embraces constructivism and explicit instruction as a trainer. He coaches nationally and internationally, producing significant increases in student and teacher outcomes both academically and affectively.

Tamarra Osborne is a project manager, trainer, and coach for WestEd in San Francisco, California. Born in Oakland, California, Tamarra was one of five siblings and a first-generation college graduate. She earned a degree in early childhood, and after a brief period teaching English in Japan, she launched her leadership and early care career. Those under Tamarra's leadership know her as an effervescent trainer and technical coach who sees the heart of a problem and provides sensible, warm-hearted solutions. Tamarra delivers training and coaching in multiple locales—from California and China to Minnesota and Missouri. Her popular conference training topics include formative assessment, curriculum development, presentation skills, implicit bias, and educational technology. Tamarra is proud to be published in NAEYC's *Young Children* magazine.

As coaches for coaches and education administrators, we work in over 2,000 classrooms in a typical year, from preschools to universities, and regularly witness some of the best teaching in the world. Those experiences informed the first book we coauthored: *The Instructional Coaching Handbook*. With more than 30 years of experience in education, we've attended and conducted countless educational workshops from Faridpur (Bangladesh) and Doha (Qatar) to Harrods Creek (Kentucky) and Shonto (Arizona). Decades of working in diverse environments provided us with a rich background of experiences in cultures where English is not the first language. We combined our training experiences and the expertise of savvy trainers with whom we've worked into *this* small and powerful book.

Related ASCD Resources: Training and Coaching

At the time of publication, the following resources were available (ASCD stock numbers in parentheses).

The Artisan Teaching Model for Instructional Leadership: Working Together to Transform Your School by Kenneth Baum and David Krulwich (#116041)

Building Teachers' Capacity for Success: A Collaborative Approach for Coaches and School Leaders by Pete Hall and Alisa A. Simeral (#109002)

The Coach Approach to School Leadership: Leading Teachers to Higher Levels of Effectiveness by Jessica Johnson, Shira Leibowitz, and Kathy Perret (#117025)

The Definitive Guide to Instructional Coaching: Seven Factors for Success by Jim Knight (#121006)

Educational Coaching: A Partnership for Problem Solving by Cathy A. Toll (#118027)

Evaluating Instructional Coaching: People, Programs, and Partnership by Sharon Thomas, Jim Knight, Michelle Harris, and Ann Hoffman (#122039)

The Instructional Coaching Handbook: 200+ Troubleshooting Strategies for Success by A. Keith Young, Angela Bell Julien, and Tamarra Osborne (#123022)

Instructional Coaching in Action: An Integrated Approach That Transforms Thinking, Practice, and Schools by Ellen B. Eisenberg, Bruce P. Eisenberg, Elliott A. Medrich, and Ivan Charner (#117028)

Learning from Coaching: How do I work with an instructional coach to grow as a teacher? by Nina Morel (#SF114066)

Peer Coaching to Enrich Professional Practice, School Culture, and Student Learning by Pam Robbins (#115014)

For up-to-date information about ASCD resources, go to www.ascd.org. You can search the complete archives of *Educational Leadership* at www.ascd.org/el.

ASCD myTeachSource®
Download resources from a professional learning platform with hundreds of research-based best practices and tools for your classroom at http://myteachsource.ascd.org.

For more information, send an email to member@ascd.org; call 1-800-933-2723 or 703-578-9600; send a fax to 703-575-5400; or write to Information Services, ASCD, 2800 Shirlington Road, Suite 1001, Arlington, Virginia USA.